Ur The Champion

The Athlete's Guide To
Reaching Your Full Potential
While Enjoying Your Sport More Than Ever Before

Denny Dicke

www.UnleashtheChampion.com

Testimonials

*"Many people think of Mr. Dicke as a coach, friend, inspirational speaker, therapist, comedian, etc. The truth is he is all of those things and much more. I learned that he can take a nervous wreck, low confidence athlete, and help them to **find the champion in their very own heart**. That alone is better than any gold medal or trophy. Countless times he would aid me in turning a very bad outlook into one that I was amazed I even had."*

Lauren Clark
State Champion
Penn State University Graduate

"Denny Dicke was the first one to mold my mental strength into what it is today. He first helped me win the State Meet and had a huge impact on helping me accomplish breaking the Four Minute Mile which is what Sports Illustrated calls "The Greatest Sporting Accomplishment of the 20th Century." As a former athlete, father and businessman he has the perfect background for what it takes to mold the minds of many of America's future stars to not only help them reach their immediate goals, but to have an impact on their careers and family life."

Chris Estwanik
State Champion
Olympic Trial Finalist
Wake Forest University Graduate

"Mr. Dicke is truly one of the most amazing people I have ever met. As a coach, friend and an invaluable role model in my life, he has taught me so many important things on how to become a successful athlete. When I first came out for track and field my senior year, I was completely in the dark on the mental aspects of sports. But Mr. Dicke changed all of that. His positive outlook and mental drills were able to take a kid who had never played a high school sport to the heights of first team All State and a national championship. Mr. Dicke's books and teachings will transform you from thinking that certain things are just not possible to knowing that the sky is the limit."

Ryan Blake
All-State
Junior College National Champion

"Mr. Dicke has done so much for me. The extra motivation and coaching were incredible. I remember one instance when I was so disappointed after finishing seventh in the State Cross Country meet and Mr. Dicke talked with me and quickly worked wonders for my confidence. I went on to run two great races in the Mid West Championship and Nationals. I guess all I needed was to believe in myself again and he helped me to do that."

Marni Kruppa
State Champion
National Champion
Three Time Collegiate All American
Georgetown University Graduate

iii

"Every athlete and coach at any level will benefit from this book. The message applies to weekend warriors or world class athletes; to athletes in youth leagues or major leagues. The techniques taught in this book will help athletes build a strong foundation for mental strength. Denny has a unique ability to take what he learned over his athletic career and pass it on to others. He knows how to teach, how to motivate and how to get the best out of people."

Dr. Mike Thomson
"America's #1 Character Coach"
Speaker/Author/Consultant
www.itsallaboutcharacter.com

Unleash The Champion

The Athlete's Guide To
Reaching Your Full Potential
While Enjoying Your Sport More Than Ever Before

All Rights Reserved © 2007 by
Dennis F. Dicke

UTC Publishing

ISBN: 978-0-9795490-0-7

Cover Design by Neal Carter

Printed in the United States of America

www.Unleashthechampion.com

Dedication

This book is dedicated to my wife Janice who has inspired me beyond measure and has gifted me with the joy of a happy and loving marriage. It is also dedicated to my three children Kevin, Erin and Kyle who I cherish and who have given me the opportunity to experience one of life's greatest treasures...that of being a Dad. I dedicate this book to my parents as well. Although they are no longer living, their positive influence on my life has been immeasurable.

Acknowledgements

First and foremost I would like to thank my parents for being the greatest coaches a person could have. Neither one of them ever played an organized sport yet their teachings made me a better athlete, coach and person.

I would like to thank all of the coaches I have had over the years. From youth leagues to middle school to high school to college to graduate school and while training for the Olympic Trials. I look back and realize that every one of my coaches had a significant positive impact and taught me lessons that apply to all areas of life not just sports. Without their positive influence this book would never have been written.

I would also like to thank all of the teammates I have had during my athletic career. Those relationships are the greatest trophies a person can receive.

Finally I would like to thank all of the athletes who I have had the privilege to coach. I have learned so much from each of them, but most importantly they made me realize that helping them reach their goals was even more exhilarating than achieving my own goals.

Please Share

Your reactions to this book would be greatly appreciated. Please let me know what had the most impact on you and specifically how your athletic performance was affected. Please visit the website **www.unleashthechampion.com** to contact me. This web site is designed to help athletes reach their goals and to provide an ongoing source of motivation. To assure its effectiveness your feedback regarding the web site would be helpful as well.

Contents

Introduction

Ryan went out for track for the first time during his senior year in high school. After learning the techniques taught in this book he became District Champion and All State. The next year as a freshman in college he became National Champion in his event. Ryan came to realize that succeeding in his event was something that he not only believed he could do, but was something that he totally enjoyed doing. He learned how to *unleash the champion.*

Another young man named Chris was a very talented athlete and in previous years he would win all of his races prior to the State Meet in Cross Country and Track. However, when the State Meet would come around, he would fold and perform much worse than expected. During his senior track season we worked on many of the things available to you in this book. In the State Meet he became a dual State Champion. He finally reached his potential at just the right time. Later in his career he became one of the elite runners to break the four minute mile. He also was a surprise qualifier for the 1500 meter finals in the 2004 Olympic Trials. He learned how to *unleash the champion.*

Every time I recall memories such as those mentioned above I realize what a wonderful time I have had working with athletes over the last thirty years. My sincere intention with this book is that you will be impacted in a similar positive way.

My own athletic career included the following accomplishments. In high school I was the starting running back on our football team which won two State Championships. I was also captain of the varsity basketball team. In track I was a three time State Champion and All American. Over 35 years later I still hold my high school's record in the 200 and the 400 meters. In college I focused on track and became conference champion in the 400 meters, was voted most valuable track athlete and achieved All American status. I mention these accomplishments because I believe that I was able to reach my full potential in athletics and it was probably 70% due to the mental conditioning and 30% due to the physical conditioning. I am convinced that the mental training is what gave me a huge edge over what someone with my same physical characteristics could have done.

Because of my passion for sports and working with young people I found time to coach football, soccer, softball, baseball, basketball and track and field. Working with athletes confirmed what I learned as an athlete. **What goes on between your ears has much more impact on your athletic performance than your level of talent or physical fitness.**

The material in this book applies to **all athletes regardless of age, gender, experience, skill level or sport.**

This book is a must read for coaches as well. Consider this book your coach's manual for mental conditioning. All coaches talk about the importance of the mental side of the game, but how many coaches actually have effective tools to teach their athletes? Within this book coaches will find proven techniques so they can coach mental conditioning and improve their athlete's performance.

Remember, you will get out of this material what you put into it. Do the exercises, answer the questions, be creative, take your time, relax and know that you can be better at your sport than you are today and at the same time you can truly enjoy your sport more than ever before. Yes, you can reach your full potential. **Yes, you can *Unleash The Champion.***

Chapter One

<u>Goals</u>

In this chapter you will learn about a very powerful goal setting method. This isn't your typical boring goal setting session. **If you set your goals with the specific technique given in this chapter you will gain an edge and have a great foundation for reaching your full potential.** Effective goal setting is the critical first step.

If an archer takes out his bow and arrow and starts shooting it all over the place would that accomplish anything? Maybe he had some fun and got some exercise, but he never hit a target because there simply wasn't one to hit. Unfortunately, I see a lot of athletes start a season without establishing any targets and they rarely accomplish anything significant. It would be as if you were driving around in your car and you get lost, so you stop when you see a policeman and say, "Excuse me, can you give me directions?" And the policeman says, "Sure, where do you want to go." Then there is this long pause and you look at him and say, "I don't have a clue!!" See how foolish that is? It is even more foolish if you go through all the hard physical training for your sport for three to nine months and don't have a clue about what you are trying to accomplish.

Think for a moment how accommodating your mind is. It has an incredible ability to bring to your attention things that you are interested in and to delete things that you are not interested in. I remember when one of my sons got his drivers license he decided he wanted to use the money he had made to buy a car. I asked him why and he explained with no uncertain terms about how great it would be to have a car. Then I asked him some questions like make, model, year, mileage, service record, price range and he got very specific. Suddenly both he and I started to see and hear advertisements for cars that we had never noticed before. There was a car parked in a parking lot and one in someone's driveway with "For Sale" signs on them. We had driven down these roads many times before so we thought these cars just came up for sale. After we called we found out that the cars had been there for a few months. We never noticed them until we decided to buy a car. We even started to notice other cars on the road. It was as if the entire town had turned into an auto mall designed to help my son determine exactly which type of car to buy. Mysteriously about a week or two after the car was purchased, all of the car advertisements and "For Sale" signs disappeared. The signs did not actually go away. What happened was our minds deleted this information because it was no longer useful or important.

This is such a critically important concept that I want to review the basics here and even give it a name –
The Attention Factor:

> ➤ Your mind wants to be **told** what it is that you think is important enough to get its attention.
> ➤ Your mind wants to be **shown** what it is that you think is important enough to get its attention.
> ➤ Your mind wants to be **convinced with emotion** that what you desire is important enough to get its attention.
> ➤ Your mind will **delete everything else**.

Now that you know this truth about how you are wired, use it to the full extent in your sport. For athletes that perform tasks requiring precision such as hitting a golf ball, pitching a baseball, bowling, high jumping or kicking field goals their performance can be improved a great deal by understanding and applying the principles of *The Attention Factor*. For example, a golfer that is faced with an approach shot over a lake. The worst thing she can do is to say to herself or hear someone say to her, "Don't hit it in the water". Her mind is designed to help her hit the ball where her attention is focused and to ignore everything else. Because "the water" was the image she created, her mind will help her to hit it in the lake.

When a manager of a baseball team calls a time out to go talk to his pitcher, unfortunately he may say to him, "Don't walk this guy", or worse yet, "You better not walk this guy or I'll bench you." Those statements create a very clear image to walk the batter. The second comment also invokes an image of sitting on the bench and feeling rejected. In this situation the brain will do all that it can to help the pitcher walk the batter and end up on the bench.

It is very natural for a coach to talk to an athlete in the way mentioned above with the pitcher. It seems perfectly logical to tell the athlete to avoid making a mistake. But if the coach will remember *The Attention Factor* and realize that he needs to use words that create successful images, he will have a positive impact on the athlete's performance.

Field goal kickers are amazing because their talents are used sparingly, but their impact on the team's success is enormous. Many times when the kickers are ready to attempt a game winning field goal, the opposing team calls a time out. You will hear the announcers say that, "They are trying to freeze the kicker", or "They are giving him time to think about it." Unfortunately, if the kicker doesn't understand *The Attention Factor* he may let his mind be lured into thoughts, images and emotions of missing the field goal. His mind will then accommodate.

It is of extreme importance for precision athletes to understand *The Attention Factor* and use it to their advantage. Golfers should focus only on the green on that approach shot. Forget about everything else including the mechanics of your swing. Save the mechanics for the practice tee. It is time to put the ball on the green and that is the only thing your mind should be focused on. Pitchers should focus their attention on exactly where in the strike zone that next pitch is going to go. Bowlers should see all the pins falling down. High Jumpers should see themselves in the pit with the bar still standing. Field goal kickers should see the football going right between the uprights. If the other team calls time out, just laugh to yourself because all they are doing is giving you more time to solidify your outcome in your mind.

Now let's apply *The Attention Factor* to every type of athlete (not just the precision athletes) and understand how important it is when setting goals.

I had a wonderful high school football coach who I will refer to many times because he was such a great teacher and motivator. In his last three years of coaching he won three State Championships in a row. I can't even count the number of times I heard him say, **"SEE CLEARLY"** when referring to what we wanted to accomplish. Before we went out for our first practice, we sat in the gymnasium and he told us to come up with a goal for the team as well as individually for the season. Then every week during the season he would set team goals that applied to our next game. There were no more than two goals and they were very clear and simple. One of the coaches would draw pictures of the weekly goals on a big poster that would hang in the locker room as a daily reminder. So the key is to have a goal for yourself and the team for the season and to have short term goals prior to every competition.

The following is the most effective goal setting method I have ever used. It is powerful because it is a three step process that combines CLARITY with EMOTION and ACTION.

Step 1: *GOAL*

In setting your goal you must follow four rules:

1. ***Use past tense***. State your goal as if you have already achieved it

2. ***Be very specific***. Include exactly what you have achieved, where you achieved it, when you achieved it and any other important specifics.

3. ***No limits***. State your goal in such a way that there are no limits on your performance.

4. ***Fun***. Express how much fun you had accomplishing your goal.

Here are some examples of effective goal setting:

Do *not* say:
"I want to rush for 1,000 yards."

What's wrong?
- It is not clear as to when you want to achieve this goal.
- It is not clear what team you are on.
- It says "I want". It is not stated as if it has already happened.
- It limits you to 1,000 yards.
- There is no fun factor.

Instead say:
"In the 2007 football season for Fairbanks High School I rushed for over 1,000 yards and totally had fun doing it."

Do *not* say:
"I wish that I score 20 goals for my team this year"
What's wrong?
- It is not clear as to when. "This year" is not clear enough.
- It says "I wish".
- It limits you to 20 goals.
- It is not specific as to what team.
- There is no fun factor.

Instead say:
"In the 2008 fall soccer season for Ross College I scored over 19 goals and completely enjoyed every minute of it."

Before you write down your goal consider what John McKissick, the football coach who has won more games than any coach (as of 12/31/06 he has won 543 games), has to say about setting goals, **"Set your goals a little out of reach, but not out of sight."** To follow his advice, do the following exercise:

Goals

In the first column below, write down specifically what your current best performance is in your sport. In the next column write down what you would consider to be a "Good" performance for this season and then finally write down what you would consider to be a "Great" performance in the third column. Now split the difference between "Good" and "Great" and use that as the minimum goal level. It is a good idea to ask your coach for assistance with this process, but ultimately this is your decision. This must be your goal and no one else's, so you write down the final answers.

For example a high school 400 meter runner's best time last year was 52 seconds. If he is writing his goal for the season, he might think that 50 seconds would be "Good" and 49 seconds would be "Great". Splitting the difference between 49 and 50 is 49.5, so his goal statement would say, "In the 2008 track season for Superior High School I ran *under 49.6* seconds in the 400 meter run, totally smashed my old record and felt awesome doing it!"

Or a professional baseball player who had a .290 batting average might think that an average of .310 would be "Good" for this season and ".350" would be great. Splitting the difference between .310 and .350 would be .330, so his goal statement would say, "In the 2007 Major League Baseball season, I totally enjoyed playing for The St. Louis Cardinals and my batting average was over .329."

Fill in the columns and then take the time right now to complete your Goal Statement for the season for your individual performance.

Current	Good	Great

Please stop reading and write down your personal goal for this season. You may do this on a separate piece of paper or for your convenience there is a page at the end of this chapter you can use.

Now that you have written down your goal another effective thing you can do is to draw a picture of yourself accomplishing the goal or find a picture in a magazine that best depicts you accomplishing your goal. Position that picture in a place where you will see it everyday such as your bathroom mirror or your bedroom wall. **Making a picture of your goal is an effective tool because it helps you consistently create this picture in your mind.**

Step 2: *WHY*

On the same piece of paper write down various reasons WHY it is so important that you reach your goal. Be very illustrative. Use convincing and descriptive terms. Explain

WHY it would be so incredibly exciting to achieve your goal. If you say, "It would be good", you will fall asleep with boredom. Instead if you say something like, "When I achieved my goal I felt so incredibly proud" or "I felt like I was walking on air, flying above the clouds, I was so unbelievably excited. It was the best feeling in the world." Now you have your mind's attention. Humans simply perform better when they have a strong cause. There is a piece of wisdom that says, "If there is a strong enough why, you will find a way." So get involved with this exercise and develop a strong cause within you that is the purpose behind your goal.

Please stop reading now and write all the reasons why you want to achieve your goal. Do this on the same piece of paper as you wrote your goal or at the end of this chapter.

Step 3: *ACTION*

On the same piece of paper write down all of the steps that you know you need to take to reach your goal. After you are done with your list, go back and prioritize the action steps by numbering them. The first step should always be to set short term goals for each up-coming competition. The second step should always be to be consistent about your mental conditioning. After you have read this entire book, you should go back to your action list and add the tools that you have learned. Your physical training, diet and amount of sleep should also be on this action list. After you are done writing down your action steps make sure that you do the first step NOW. Drop everything, including this book and do that first step now. Immediately after you get the first step completed reward yourself. This will get your momentum going and you will be on your way to success.

To give you an example of the goal setting process the following is what was written by a high school senior track athlete a week before the State Meet. This is the same person I referred to in the introduction. Chris was very talented but simply did not perform well in the most important races. During his senior track season, one of the techniques we worked on was effective goal setting. The week before the State Meet he wrote the following:

Goal: "On June 6, 1998 at 9:55 A.M. I became the State Champion in the 1600 meter run!"

Why: "The glory.

I deserve it after all the hard work that I have put in these last 4 years.

Because it would be the most thrilling, magnificent, feeling that I have ever experienced in my life.

This is for myself, my friends, my school, my family, my coaches, and anyone else who took the time to help me during these last 4 years.

Because it would be the greatest memory to have in the future."

Action: "Run relaxed at my pace then with 300 meters to go - all out kick past everyone."

When race day came I went up to Chris and gave him a quick shot of encouragement by simply saying, "You can do it". He looked at me with a smile of confidence and said, "I got it". Then he went out and did it. It was exciting to see him run the exact race he had described to me earlier. With 300 meters to go he was in fourth place and about 40 yards behind the leader. He took off, ran the other guys down, passed the leader on the last curve and finished first. He ran his best time ever and broke the school record. **Most importantly this was a great mental breakthrough for this gifted athlete. He finally ran free. He *unleashed the champion*.**

This young man went on to run in college and after college he kept training and became one of the elite runners to break the four - minute mile. In the 2004 Olympic Trials he was a surprising qualifier to the finals in the 1500 meter run. What this tells me is that he continued to set his sights high. Why not? When you are not afraid, but instead have found a love for the sport, you can reach as high as you desire.

<u>The Three Step Goal Setting Process</u>

Goal:

Why:

Action:

Chapter Two

<u>Identity</u>

A critical part of performing up to your full potential is to have a high degree of certainty about the characteristics you aspire to have in order to reach your goal. There are two steps for coming up with your identity.

Step 1:

Review the Goal that you have for yourself for this season. If you need help with clarifying your goal, go back to Chapter 1 and do the exercises. Then consider the characteristics you will need to have to accomplish this goal. On the next page is a list of 140 descriptive terms. As you go through the list decide which three are the ones that will best propel you toward your goal. Take your time and feel free to make changes. You may want to pick your top twelve first. Then whittle it down to six and then to the final three. The three terms that apply best to you will become very clear as you go through this process.

Adaptable	Consistent	Fast	Magical	Sensible
Adept	Controlled	Fearless	Magnetic	Serene
Aggressive	Cool	Focused	Make It Happen	Sincere
Agile	Cooperative	Franchise	Masculine	Skillful
Alert	Courageous	Free	Motivated	Smooth
Ambitious	Creative	Friendly	Opportunistic	Special
Assertive	Daring	Fulfilled	Optimistic	Spectacular
Aware	Decisive	Fun-Loving	Passionate	Spirited
Awesome	Determined	Genuine	Patient	Spontaneous
Balanced	Dignified	Gifted	Peaceful	Strong
Blessed	Diligent	Graceful	Playful	Successful
Bold	Disciplined	Grateful	Perfect	Super
Brave	Driven	Great	Phenomenal	Superb
Breakthrough	Dynamic	Honest	Poised	Swift
Bright	Dynamite	Humble	Positive	Talented
Brilliant	Effective	Incredible	Powerful	Tenacious
Calculating	Empowered	Important	Prime Time	Terrific
Capable	Energetic	Independent	Pumped-Up	Tremendous
Centered	Enthusiastic	Industrious	Psyched-Up	Trusting
Charismatic	Exciting	Inspirational	Purposeful	Trustworthy
Cheerful	Exhilarating	Inspired	Quick	Turbo-Charged
Classy	Explosive	Intelligent	Relaxed	Unique
Coachable	Extraordinary	Intense	Reliable	Unselfish
Competent	Exuberant	Intuitive	Resourceful	Unstoppable
Competitive	Fabulous	Invincible	Responsible	Vibrant
Complete	Faithful	Joyful	Responsive	Well-Conditioned
Composed	Fantastic	Limitless	Rhythmic	Wonderful
Confident	Fascinating	Loyal	Self-Controlled	Worthy

Step 2:

After deciding on your three characteristics that will help you reach your full potential, it is time to describe yourself with these words. **The next phrase is incredibly important because it claims your identity as an athlete. To do this effectively start your phrase with two very powerful words – "I AM".** Then fill in the three blanks with the three terms you have chosen to describe yourself. End the phrase with the word "athlete" or use the sport that you are involved in if that feels more appropriate. Instead of "Athlete" you would write "Football Player", "Soccer Player", "Wrestler", "Basketball Player", "Golfer", "La Crosse Player", "Swimmer", "Tennis Player", "Baseball Player" or whatever applies.

Complete your identity phrase now.

I AM a (an) _____,

_____,

& _____

ATHLETE

Display your identity phrase someplace where you can see it regularly like your bathroom mirror or your dashboard or a text book or your locker. If you want to be a little more private about it, but still see it regularly you could put it in your wallet or purse or on a credit card or driver's license. I actually made business cards for our 4 X 100 relay team one year. The cards had their name, their school and their goal to get to the State Meet with the year on it. Then in the middle of the card with big bold letters it said, "I AM FAST". They thought it was so cool to pull out their business cards and show their friends. It became a fun way for them to claim their identity and they did in fact make it to the State Meet.

The following is a very strong formula for enhancing performance:

Ingredients: Your Goal Statement (see chapter 1)
Your Identity Statement

Exercise: Memorize these two statements,
                 Stand in front of a mirror,
                 Look yourself directly in the eyes,
                 & repeat these two statements.

Training Schedule: 3 sets of 3

                 Repeat the two statements 3 times
                 Do this 3 times a day as follows:
                 1. As soon as you get out of bed
                 2. Right before your practice
                 Note: if you cannot be in a private place with
                 a mirror before practice, then simply close
                 your eyes and silently repeat the two
                 statements to yourself.
                 3. Right before you get in bed at night

Before leaving this chapter about identity I would like to
share with you the qualities that John McKissick has been
teaching to his high school football team, the Summerville
Green Wave, for over 55 years. Coach McKissick has won
over 540 football games, more than any other football coach
at any level. Obviously the man knows a lot about what it
takes to succeed. He has assigned a quality for each of the
letters in his team name as a constant reminder. After
reviewing this list you may want to adopt some of these
qualities for yourself.

Sacrifice (Team comes first)
Unselfishness (The "we" attitude)
Motivation (To uphold The Green Wave tradition)
Mental toughness (Never picturing defeat)
Energy (Giving all we have, all the time)
Repetition (Practice, practice, practice)
Victory (There is no laughter in losing – Lombardi)
Intestinal Fortitude (Guts to give all we have for 48
    minutes)
Loyalty (To the team)
Living for the fight (A burning desire to beat the other guy)
Execution (Daring to be perfect) (Playbook study)

God (Knowing we are God's project and God never fails!)
Resolve (Determination-Discipline-Desire)
Enthusiasm (Enjoying Friday nights under the lights)
Effort (Hustling till the whistle blows)
Never surrendering (Quitting is not an option)

Work (There is no substitute)
Academics (success in class leads to success in life)
Vision (seeing success even before we take the field)
Eleven and 0 (That's good – but 15-0 gets it done!)

Chapter Three

<u>Believe</u>

In this chapter you will learn some very effective tools for building your confidence.

Nothing great has ever been achieved without first believing that it can be done. But how do you train yourself to believe? One good way to build confidence is to have small successes and with each small success your belief in your ability builds. However, **the most effective tool for building confidence and belief is a technique called Visualization.**

Visualization is simply closing your eyes and day dreaming about your sporting event. I will suggest a couple of methods to try, but the first one is the exact three step method I used during my high school track career. I am convinced this Visualization technique was one of the main reasons I was able to do so well in track and eventually win three events in the State Championship.

Step 1: Every night before you fall asleep, lie in your bed, close your eyes and see yourself competing in your next event. Imagine yourself doing the very best. Break it down into small segments and imagine as much detail as possible. For example, I was a 400 meter runner, so I would first picture the stadium, then the track, then getting into the blocks, then starting and running the first curve, then the backstretch, then the second curve, then the homestretch and finally crossing the finish line. I would see the color of the track. I would hear people cheering for me. I would feel myself floating effortlessly and powerfully with perfect running form. I would see myself finishing strong and winning the race (which was my goal). I would feel the exhilaration of winning.

Step 2: As soon as you wake up in the morning, picture the same scene again. It is very important that this is your first thought after you come out of your sleep. Your sub-conscience is pretty much wide open and easily accessible right when you wake up, so it is best to create this positive image of yourself at that time.

Step 3: The early evening before the competition, go to the site of your athletic event and watch yourself perform just as you have been seeing it every night and morning before. If it is not possible for you to go to the site the evening before, then simply do step 1 and step 2 again and you will be fine.

By the time the day of your athletic event occurs you will wake up and feel like it is Christmas morning. You will feel a sense of great anticipation that you cannot wait to get started and do what you have already seen happen many times before. That's confidence. That's a strong sense of belief which your mental conditioning has instilled in you.

I reviewed the goal setting process in chapter 1 and this visualization technique with a high school sprinter named Allen the night before the District Championship. Afterwards I went to the track and was not surprised to see him drive up. He was getting ready to do step 3. We sat together at the finish line and he watched his race. The next day he ran with complete confidence and reached his full potential which for him was winning the 100 meters and tying the school record.

Another real life example and one of my favorites is about the high school senior named Ryan who I mentioned in the introduction. Ryan was a good basketball player, but was disappointed that he never made the high school team. Finally in the spring of his senior year he decided to go out for track just for something to do. When I saw him at the track he told me that he had decided to high jump. Although I didn't know anything about high jumping, we agreed that I might be able to help him with the mental side of the event.

Ryan had a very good coach that helped him with technique, so I just tried to help him feel confident that he could get over the bar. The day before his event Ryan would write his goal for the next day so he was clear on his intention. Then I would guide him through a visualization of accomplishing his goal. Ryan had told me his favorite pump up song was the same song that the Chicago Bulls used during their introduction of players. Also his favorite color was red, favorite thing to feel was silk, favorite smell was a special lotion and his favorite thing to taste was a Chipotle chicken burrito. During the visualization I incorporated all of his favorite things so that his brain would link up high jumping with pleasure. Through the visualization process, going over the bar became something that he not only believed he could do, but something that he totally enjoyed doing.

Ryan's results were incredible for a first year athlete in a highly technical event like high jumping. His best jump was 6'6" and he became the District Champion, took third in the Regionals and eighth in the State Championship to achieve All-State status. It was thrilling to see Ryan stand proudly on the podium at the State Meet with his medal around his neck. He had finally made a name for himself in high school athletics. When Ryan was a freshman in college I received a call from him and he was excited to tell me that he had just won the National Championship for his division. He said he had gone through the same visualization process he learned last spring and that even though this was the National Championship he felt incredibly strong, competitive, and confident and totally enjoyed the event.

Another visualization technique that requires a little more creativity is something I call *"Full Potential Theater"*. Here are the steps to go through while sitting in a comfortable chair or lying in your bed with your eyes closed.

Step 1: Imagine yourself walking into a place that you remember being one of the most beautiful and peaceful places you have ever seen. This could be somewhere you have been before, seen in a magazine, on a website, or remember from a movie or television show. It could be a beach scene, a mountain scene, a forest scene, a room in a cottage, whatever comes to your mind. Just make sure that you feel calm and happy in this place and that you spend enough time vividly remembering the colors, aroma, sights, sounds and how peaceful it makes you feel.

Step 2: As you walk through this place you come upon a door with a sign above it that says *"Full Potential Theater"*. You walk in and it is this nice movie theater with a chair for you to sit in and watch the movie. You smile and sit down in the soft and relaxing chair. Then you click the start button on the remote.

Step 3: On the screen in front of you create a movie of yourself performing to your fullest potential in your next athletic event. Be as creative as possible and sit back and enjoy the show.

Step 4: When the movie is over, get up and walk out of the theater and slowly open your eyes.

If you are unable to see the pictures you want after trying all of these methods of visualization you may be having difficulty guiding your imagination. My first suggestion is to keep trying. This is such a valuable tool that it is worth practicing until you start to feel more comfortable with it. You might try some exercises to warm up your imagination. One such exercise is to close your eyes and say out loud the names of colors and then picture a wall or a flower that becomes that color as you say it.

If after a couple weeks of sincere attempts it isn't working for you, then simply do your visualization with your eyes open. I can remember as a kid I would spend hours alone on an outdoor basketball court in any kind of weather. Instead of just shooting around I would make up game situations and would be my own announcer. "It's the first game of the tournament. He's at the free throw line with the game tied and one second left on the clock. He shoots. It's in! The fans go crazy!" This type of "eyes wide open" visualization is close to what happens when a football team or a basketball team does a "Walk Through" the day before a game. They don't just sit in a locker room and go over certain strategies; they actually walk through or jog through what they want to do in different situations. I encourage coaches to take the "Walk Through" beyond just a review process. Have the players actually carry through with accomplishing their task such as scoring a touchdown or making that basket or winning that race and then acting out the celebration that occurs afterward. The more everything can seem like game day the better.

Another effective method for visualizing your performance is to have someone guide you through the process. This person should be someone you trust who knows you and your event well. A coach would be a perfect candidate. Also, you could use a tape recorder and record your voice or someone else guiding you through your performance.

Remember one of the main reasons to visualize is to build your confidence. The key is to go through your performance over and over again so that your desired result has already occurred in your mind many times. Then when it comes time to actually perform, you will be much more confident because your mind is convinced that this is familiar ground.

I will close this chapter with a memory that I have that emphasizes the power of believing. I was coaching my son's basketball team and we made it to the final game of the tournament. We were to play the most talented team in the league that was coached by a former college star player and whose son was the top scorer in the league. I knew we were in trouble when my own son told me that we were going to get trounced. I announced to all the players and parents that we were going to have our banquet the night *before* the game. Everyone got together and we did what should be done at banquets. We had each boy stand up and we praised everything about that young man. We recalled every great shot, every great steal, every great rebound, literally every great play we could possibly remember. We praised each boy for all of his positive qualities such as his work ethic, his enthusiasm, his confidence and on and on.

By the time we were finished every boy on that team thought they were the next best thing to Michael Jordan. Then I started to talk about the game the next day in terms as if the victory had already occurred. I didn't say, "If we win tomorrow" but instead I said in no uncertain terms, "After we win tomorrow". I encouraged the parents to talk to their boys the same way. For one evening and one day there would be no "If" in our vocabulary. As it turned out every boy played the game of their life and did end up champions. It was a great victory, but it was an even greater lesson about the power of believing.

Chapter Four

<u>Voices</u>

What you say to yourself will have a huge impact on your performance. The following are four tools to help you get control over your inner voices.

1.) **Awareness**

The first critical step in gaining control over your voices is to become aware of what you are saying to yourself. The best way to do this is to use the form at the end of this section or simply use a piece of paper and draw two columns with the headings "Up" and "Down". Now *think about your upcoming sporting event and listen carefully to your thoughts.* In the "Up" column write down all of the thoughts that are positive, empowering, and encouraging. In the "Down" column list all of the thoughts that are negative, weakening, and discouraging. It is very important that you don't judge yourself while doing this exercise. You are not doing this to get a grade. You are not trying to impress anyone, because no one is going to see this list. What you are striving for is honesty…a list of what your true thoughts really are without categorizing them as right or wrong. If at one sitting you have trouble thinking of what you are saying to yourself, make note of your thoughts during the course of the day as you think about your next sporting event. The amazing thing about this process is that sometimes once you have taken the time to identify the "Down" voices it weakens them and they go away. It's as if the negative thoughts grow stronger in the dark, but once they are exposed either by writing them down or by talking to someone about them they start to diminish.

As you *think about your upcoming athletic event* if you have more than two thoughts on the "Down" side and feel you need more help, then go to step 2. Anything on your "Down" list is like heavy baggage that is weighing you down and hindering you from performing up to your fullest potential. If those negative thoughts do not diminish simply by becoming aware of them then you need to take further steps to set yourself free.

Use the next page as your guide to becoming aware of your thoughts about your next athletic event.

Voices

Up	Down

2.) **Laugh**

I learned this technique when I was a quarter-miler on my college's track team. As part of our training in the fall the coaches would have everybody run a two mile race for time around the perimeter of the campus every Friday. Everyone including throwers, vaulters, hurdlers, and jumpers had to run this race. The distance runners loved it and everyone else including me hated it. But we all had to do it. The race would start and my voices would begin, "Ok take it easy, you're a quarter-miler, you can't run very fast for a whole two miles." At the quarter mile mark, the inner thought would be, "That is as far as you are used to racing, you'd better slow down now." When some distance runner would pass me I'd say, "There's no way I can keep up with that guy, he's a distance runner." About a mile out my thought would be something like, "I really hate this. I can't believe we have to do this." As I struggled to finish the last quarter mile I would say, "My lungs are going to explode. I won't be able to walk after this. Just get me back to the dorm so I can collapse."

Finally after about two Fridays of agony, I thought about what I was saying to myself. I knew that I wasn't going to get out of doing this horrible task, so maybe it would be a little better if I didn't allow myself to think while I was doing it. I decided to have some fun with it. During the next two mile race **I was very alert to any thought that passed through my mind and if it was a negative voice I would immediately laugh it away.** For example, when I would start to hear one of the negative voices, I would laugh inside my head and while still laughing say, "Stop with this nonsense and get out of here." **Imagine if you were trying to have a serious conversation with someone and before you could finish your first sentence that person started** laughing at you and told you to leave. **That would hurt and you probably couldn't wait to get out of there. After all, that person isn't taking you seriously. That person isn't giving you any credibility at all. That is exactly how you want Mr. Negatory to feel. You want him to leave, so laugh at him.** In that two mile race I beat all of the non-distance runners and most importantly I performed to my fullest potential while feeling great during the race and afterwards. It is a freeing experience when you cut the anchors lose and just sail along doing what needs to be done in the most enjoyable fashion possible.

Another effective way to laugh out the negative baggage is to repeat back the negative thought you just heard in the most ridiculous sounding voice you could ever come up with. It is similar to a child's reaction to a bully trying to harass him with a demeaning remark. Instead of letting the bully continue, he stops him by repeating the words back to him in the most hideous sounding voice. For example, your inner voice says, "You're a big loser; you'll never be any good." You fire back in a high shrill hysterical voice, "Oh watch out everybody the bully is puking words out of his mouth like you're a big loser and you'll never be any good." Keep firing away until you start laughing because what is coming out of your mouth sounds so ridiculously funny. All of a sudden the bully puts his tail between his legs, leaves and you feel great. This technique may sound absurd, but sometimes the more absurd, the more effective. Besides it is no more absurd than taking seriously the message of the bully.

3.) **Toughness**

Another technique that works with getting rid of negative voices is to get tough with them. **Take on the attitude of**

standing guard at the door of your mind as if you were guarding the most precious treasure in the world. Be alert and if you start to hear a thief coming your way, yell at it with your utmost force. You can't allow it to get a foot in the door. You must stop it immediately. Stand tall, stand strong and with your loudest inner voice tell the thief to leave. Shout something like, "No, get out of here now. You will not have your way with me." Have some fun with this technique. Imagine that a thief was trying to get into your house. You are there alone and there are no phones. It is just you and the thief. You know that thief will leave if you shout at him in a very strong voice with very strong words. What would you say? Go to a place where you can shout without people thinking you are crazy and start shouting. If you just can't get yourself to shout out loud, then spend a little time with silent screaming. Take 30 seconds and scream as loud and as angrily as you can in your head. Even open your mouth and go through all the body motions you would do if you were really screaming at someone out loud. Then write down some of your favorite tough phrases so you can use them on that inner thief if you need them.

4.) **Kindness**

If the first three techniques were not effective, try kindness. **There is an old saying, "Kill them with kindness", and this method works with negative thoughts as well.** When Mr. Negatory comes knocking, recognize him and welcome him in. Thank him for showing up and talk to him as if he were an old friend that you haven't seen in awhile. "It's great to see you. How have you been? I've missed you. Can I get you anything? Can you stay for awhile?" For some reason when there is no resistance, but kindness instead, the negative thought goes away. It's as if those negative thoughts enjoy a fight and thrive on conflict. However, if they are greeted with kindness they go away.

~ ~ ~ ~

A good example about the power of voices was Tiger Woods during the 2005 Masters Championship. Tiger was leading going into the last two holes and he bogeyed both of them to finish in a tie. Instead of saying something demeaning to himself such as, "How could you blow a two shot lead with two holes to go?" He revealed that during the playoff he heard his Dad's voice in his head saying, "Trust your swing" and "Pick out your spot." These types of phrases got him back on track and lead him to another Masters victory.

~~~~~~

While on the subject of Voices, three topics need to be reviewed: Questions, Pain, and Competition.

Questions

Another very important part of being aware of your voices is to listen for any Questions you may be asking and determine if they would go in the "Up" column or the "Down" column. **Questions are powerful. Imagine for a moment that every question you ask yourself has an answer. After all, your brain is like a computer and if you ask it something it will search for an answer. Be very careful about the questions you find yourself asking and if it is something demeaning, quickly erase it by changing the question to something empowering.**

Pain

The type of pain I am referring to is pain caused by exhaustion, not pain caused by an injury. Most sports push an athlete to experience some level of pain due to exhaustion either in their practices or their events or both. When this pain level is reached it is perfectly normal for your brain to react to protect you. It will signal thoughts to stop the activity that is causing the pain. The problem is that if you stop or slow down you will never improve. **The exciting thing to realize is that we can raise that threshold of pain by concentrating on our voices when the exhaustion starts to slow us down.** Use the four methods discussed above to breakthrough the weakening thoughts brought on by pain. It also helps to change your perception of pain. I remember hearing my coaches constantly reminding me with phrases such as, "Yes you can", "You're getting stronger", "You're putting money in the bank", "Now is when you are going to start getting something out of this workout", "It's time to breakthrough" or "You love this hill". I hope you have coaches that are there to replace your weak thoughts with strong thoughts. It is such an important role for a coach to observe his athletes carefully and when they start to weaken physically, they replace the athlete's voices with a different perception of that pain they are experiencing. If you don't have a coach, know for sure that you can train yourself to increase your pain threshold.

If you are involved in a sport where there is no physical exhaustion, you can practice overcoming pain by designing some physical workouts that will help you reach an exhaustion level. For you, this has nothing to do with physical conditioning, but is purely for strengthening your mind. Running and weight lifting are two of the most common methods, although sit ups and push ups can be effective as well. Before doing the physical exercise, decide what you are going to say to your thoughts of the pain. Be alert and as soon as the pain starts to give you a warning sign, use your strategy against it. You could laugh at it, use tough words, use kind words or some catchy phrase like "I'm putting money in the bank". Remember that the sole intention of this exercise is to practice breaking through the pain. Many athletes will use their practice time to improve their skills, work on their strategy, work on flexibility, work on their form or to get a good workout in. All of this is important, but for strengthening the mind their needs to be more. Set aside some time for the specific purpose of breaking through pain caused by physical exhaustion. **You should approach these exercises with a sense of excitement because you know that when the pain arrives you are going to meet it with a powerful force - your imagination - and you are going to feel exhilarated when you break through.**

Competition

It is extremely important to have a healthy attitude about your competition. The only way to do this is to first know what your thoughts are about the competition you are about to face. What is your inner voice really saying to you about the opponent?

What if the opponent is ranked lower or clearly has less talent than you?

One of the main reasons why upsets happen is because the higher ranked team or athlete did not have a healthy attitude about their competition. They simply didn't respect their opponent and therefore they didn't prepare mentally or physically for the competition.

Athletes with a healthy attitude about their competition, first of all, have total respect for every opponent. They know that their challenger could rise to the occasion and perform better than they ever have. Secondly, the healthy minded athlete views every upcoming event as another opportunity to perform. That is what they love to do regardless of where they are or who they are up against. There is absolutely no way that they would ever even think about wasting that opportunity.

What if the opponent is ranked higher than you?

The most common debilitating voices are what I call *"Pedestal Thoughts"*. This occurs by thinking so highly of your opponents abilities that you put them on a pedestal. You elevate them to super hero, unbeatable status and you see yourself as some lowly unworthy opponent.

The healthy response is to embrace the challenge with a delightful spirit and great expectation. It's a similar response as when a child gets a favorite brand new toy for Christmas.

It goes beyond just having another opportunity to perform. The healthy minded athlete is even more excited about competing against a good opponent because they know the good opponent will help them perform at their highest level.

~~~~~

A note to coaches...

If there is just one thing that I could offer a coach as the most important bit of wisdom to embed deep in your mind it would be this: **You have incredible power!**

Your voice becomes the most dominant voice of the athlete you are coaching, therefore every message you send your athletes whether by your voice, your body language or your actions is incredibly powerful. Know this and as part of your job as a coach take full responsibility for becoming your athletes voice. Assume they don't have a voice of their own and it is your mission to fill their minds with the empowering voices that will help them achieve their full potential.

Coaches, take some time to think about this awesome power that you have and become completely aware of your messages. Maybe go to the extent of having someone video tape you during practices and games. Then review the video from a self analysis point of view. Draw two columns on a piece of paper with one titled "Up" and the other titled "Down" and write in the appropriate column every message that you gave an athlete either by your voice, your body language or your actions. Then ask yourself some interesting questions. First, put yourself in the athlete's shoes and ask how you would have been impacted if some coach that you totally respected had given you those same messages? Second, ask yourself if these messages are going to help your athletes reach their full potential? After this analysis you may see that some changes need to be made. For the sake of the individual athletes and for the sake of your team, restructure your messages and continue to monitor them in the future.

One of the most unproductive things I see some basketball coaches do is when they pull a player off the floor as soon as he makes a mistake. The coach may even add a disgusted look on his face. All of this appears to be just normal, logical behavior. The typical thinking is that if someone makes a mistake they should be pulled because they are hurting the team. If the coach looks disgusted that is just a normal human reaction. If you are a coach that uses this philosophy, please consider what I have to say. Ask yourself if you were playing for John Wooden or Phil Jackson and he pulled you out after your first mistake, what would you tell yourself? Could the message be interpreted as, "I don't trust you. I'm going to give you a little playing time here, but I'm not expecting much of anything. As soon as you make a mistake that will confirm for me that you aren't any good." Now the next time you got on the floor, are those voices the ones you want to hear? Will those voices elevate your play or diminish any hope of improvement?

What would happen if you changed your message in the following way? For this example, let's say the player's name is Tom. At every practice you pointed out everything that Tom was doing right. The night before the game you talked with Tom and told him that you really liked the way he practiced that week and you were looking forward to putting him in the game. Mention certain skills and characteristics that you saw during practice or at other times in the season and confirm how much he has improved and how much you believe in him. Then tell him that when he goes into the game you want to give him enough time to get into the flow. He should expect to give his best effort for at least five solid minutes. Tell him to just go in there, have a good time, and keep getting better every minute. Say, "After five minutes I will probably take you out to teach you something or to let someone else have the same chance to play that you had. When you come out, sit right beside me so we can talk."

See the difference? See how productive this message is to the player? His interpretation becomes, "I am worthy. I have good skills and characteristics. I am improving. Coach believes in me. I'm free to get into the flow of the game and maybe even make a mistake or two, but Coach knows I will keep getting better. When I come out he is going to teach me something because he knows I can be better."

There was an excellent article in the February 21, 2005 USA Today about Larry Brown, who at the time was the head coach of the Detroit Pistons. He has been coaching for 32 years and to mention a few of his accomplishments he won the NCAA Championship in 1988, was NBA Coach of the Year in 2001, enshrined into the Basketball Hall of Fame in 2002, won the NBA Championship in 2004 and coached the Olympic Team that same year. The title of the article sums up his key to success, "Coach says honey gets better results than vinegar." Coach Brown made the comment that when he was coaching in college, students who were doing a thesis came to their practices and recorded his responses. His ratio was 4 or 5 positive remarks to 1 negative. When the reporter asked him, "How do you address mistakes without introducing a fear of making mistakes?" he responded as follows: **"Our game is a game of mistakes. I tell our players that if you're not making mistakes, you're not trying to win. I don't want mistakes for lack of effort. But I don't want anyone to fear losing. I want them to fear not giving their best effort."**

Coaches, know your power and use it. Be the voice.

Chapter Five

<u>Now</u>

The rock group Van Halen sang an inspiring song called "Right Now" and I would highly recommend it as an effective pump up song as well as an important lesson.

The song teaches that **when you are performing your particular athletic skill, it is extremely important to keep your thoughts in the present moment.** To perform effectively you must learn that right now is all that matters. There isn't any tomorrow nor is there any yesterday. This moment right now is everything there is. This moment right now is your magic moment. Whether you are getting ready for a Lacrosse game, a Soccer game, a Rugby match, or if you are setting up to throw a shot put, do a tumbling routine, serve a tennis ball, hit a golf ball, or shoot a free throw the same truth applies. Right now is the only thing that you can do anything about, so all of your attention needs to focus on this moment right now.

My high school football coach used two specific tools to keep us focused on the present task at hand:

"Take them one at a time" – At the end of each practice he would blow his whistle and we would all run up to him shouting the number of the game on our schedule and holding the appropriate number of fingers in the air as well.

If it was the second game of the year we would shout, "Two" about twenty times while pumping two fingers in the air. He had seen too many great teams get beat by lesser opponents because they were looking past that opponent to another team later in the season. He also knew that we would simply perform better and enjoy ourselves more if we focused all of our energy and attention on the upcoming game. We would not be distracted by what had happened in the past or what would possibly happen in the future. Right now was all that mattered. As far as we were concerned we only had one game on our schedule and that was the one on the upcoming Friday night.

"Nothing to Nothing" - Whenever the offense would run off the field after scoring another touchdown, coach would yell, "What's the score?" and we would shout back, "It's nothing to nothing!", even if we were up by three or four touchdowns. He knew that in order to play our best throughout the entire game that we had to maintain our focus. He had seen too many come from behind victories and witnessed too many shifts in momentum. He knew that a, "Nothing to nothing" mindset would prevent us from letting up and would keep us in control of the game.

If we ever got behind, the same question and response applied. "What's the score?" "Nothing to nothing!" The obvious implication was to never give up. To never think we were too far behind to come back. If we kept focused on improving right now it would be the beginning of our climb back.

Your exercise for this Chapter is to come up with a key phrase to help you remember to stay in the present moment while performing your sport. "Nothing to Nothing" is my personal favorite because I have seen it work effectively in so many situations and please feel free to use it if it applies.

Please complete your *Now* phrase right now:

_____

Chapter Six

<u>Heroes</u>

My high school football coach knew the power of modeling heroes and implemented it in a very effective way. He had us watch training films. These were not just game films from previous years. He had taken all of those old films and carefully edited them into one film with all the great tackles, great blocks, great passes, great runs, great kickoff and punt returns, great interceptions, great fumble recoveries, great field goals and on and on. It was a highlight film of the best plays that players on our team from previous years had ever made. He knew that in order to reach our full potential we had to model those players that had already achieved what we wanted to accomplish.

One of the most important ingredients to reaching your full potential is to determine who the best athletes are in your sport and *who have the type of characteristics you appreciate*. Then study everything you can about those people and model all that they do. There is absolutely no reason why you should waste a lot of time and effort on trial and error. Why try to reinvent the wheel when it has already been invented. They have paved the way and now it is your job to discover how they did it. It is important to emphasize that you do not want to model just the best athletes. You must be careful to model athletes that also have the type of qualities you want to have.

If possible, make personal contact with your heroes and ask for an interview. If you believe this is someone that could help you, ask that person to mentor you throughout your season. This would involve no more than a 15 minute phone call every week or two at a scheduled time. Regardless of how busy or how uninterested you may think your heroes are, many people enjoy helping others improve and are flattered that you asked.

If your hero is popular enough to be in the media, read every magazine, newspaper article and book about them. Do a search on the internet to see if you can discover more. Try to find a movie about them. Search for a highlight DVD or training DVD. If you can, communicate with their coaches or fellow teammates. You want to know how they trained, what they ate, what their strategies were, but most importantly you want to know what they thought about and how they prepared mentally.

When I think of a modern day professional athlete who used this hero modeling concept to its full extent I think of Tiger Woods. From reading many articles and books about Tiger, I understand that he had pictures of Jack Nicklaus in his bedroom when he was a young boy. These pictures were a very clear reminder of his goal to become the best golfer in the world. He knew exactly what he intended to do and these pictures helped solidify the image for him. However, his modeling didn't stop at just pictures. He read all that he could about all the great golfers such as Ben Hogan, Arnold Palmer, Gary Player, and of course Jack Nicklaus. He spent hours watching tapes of them playing. He hired coaches that knew many of these golfers and had these coaches teach him the strategies, techniques and mental habits of these great golfers.

45

The following is the exercise for this chapter that will help you get started on this effective tool of hero modeling.

1.) Use the following table and in the second column write down three of the top athletes you can think of that ever participated in *any* sport. In the third column write down three top athletes in *your* sport and preferably those that play your position. If you can't think of people at very high levels such as the pros, then think of the top athletes who play at your level.

	Any Sport	Your Sport
Athlete 1		
Athlete 2		
Athlete 3		

For example, the following is how a college quarterback might complete this table:

	Any Sport	Your Sport
Athlete 1	Tiger Woods	Peyton Manning
Athlete 2	Michael Jordan	Tom Brady
Athlete 3	Muhammad Ali	Joe Montana

If you feel limited by the six boxes available, then write down as many names that come to mind. If you couldn't fill all of the six boxes, as long as you have three, you are ready to go on. If you need to brainstorm with other people such as your coach, please do so. This is not a test to see who you know. You just want to develop a good list of potential heroes to model, so get help if you need to.

2.) From the above table that you completed pick three names of athletes that you would benefit the most from knowing. At least one should represent your sport.

    1. _____
    2. _____
    3. _____

3.) If possible get a picture of these athletes and display them in your room. If necessary do a search on the internet for sports posters.

4.) Learn everything you can about how these athletes approached their training and their competitions from both the physical side and the mental side. Try to contact these heroes by mail and ask for a phone interview. If you do not get the interview continue to do all that you can to learn their strategies. Analyze the characteristics of these three heroes. What three words would you use to describe each of them? Then determine if you should go back to Chapter 2 and change any of your own identity statements. Truly model these heroes by studying all that you can about them and applying what you have learned to your own situation.

Chapter Seven

<u>Rituals</u>

Dictionary.com defines a ritual as, "any practice or pattern of behavior regularly performed in a set manner." It is important for athletes to develop a ritual that they do before every competition. **Regardless of what type of athlete you are, your mind likes consistency. If you give it a ritual it will serve to not only calm the mind, but to signal the mind that it is time to focus and perform. This ritual should also serve to remind yourself of a past athletic experience that you were very pleased with.**

Some people may call certain rituals "superstitious", but in reality rituals are just good sound mental conditioning. I heard that there was a Wisconsin football player that put an ace of spades in each shoe before a game. When questioned about it he simply said, "Because they are the best cards in the deck." If someone believes that the cards are going to make them play better, that's superstition. However, what this young man was doing was a very creative tool for getting his mind ready to play. As opposed to telling himself to get focused and do his best, he used a signal, the ace of spades, and consistently used the same signal. Without saying a word, his mind became conditioned to know that when the "best card" went into his shoe, it was time to respond with complete attention on playing up to his fullest potential.

Many athletes like to have the exact same pre-competition routine as they had the last time they performed their best. The night before their event they eat the same dinner and go to bed at the same time. They get up at the same time and eat the same breakfast. They listen to the same music. They talk to the same people. They look at the same things like possibly a picture or a video. They touch the same things like possibly their pet or stuffed animal or get a hug from a family member. They smell the same things like maybe a freshly laundered towel. They wear the same socks or underwear or T shirt that they wore during their last good performance. This is all very healthy for the mind for several reasons. First, the athletes are reminding themselves of the last time they performed well. Second, all of these familiar items serve to comfort their minds. Finally, these actions are flashing a green light signal that it is time to perform.

The next time you have the chance, watch a high level tennis tournament, golf tournament, or bowling tournament. Observe a baseball pitcher, a high jumper or the good free-throw shooters in a basketball game. Study the rituals that these precision athletes go through before every effort. That's the consistency and familiarity that the mind responds to with calmness and focus.

Unfortunately when observing these athletes, there is no way to see what ritual is going on inside their heads. However, the consistent mental ritual is what separates the great precision athletes from the good ones. Either they are affirming their strong characteristics (Chapter 2 – Identity), visualizing an excellent outcome (Chapter 3 - Believe), encouraging themselves with positive self-talk (Chapter 4 – Voices), humming a song to keep relaxed and rhythmic (Chapter 16 – Spirit), or whatever works for them. These are all significant tools to use as part of your ritual that are designed to calm the mind, focus the mind, build confidence, and help you be smooth and rhythmic. **It is very important to note that once it is time to perform, that all thoughts must cease.** The ritual is for preparation purposes only. When it comes time to swing the club, release the bowling ball, throw the pitch, or shoot the free throw the mind must become quiet. It must let the body perform without any more instruction or interference.

It is equally important for individuals as well as teams to have rituals. Many college football teams will wear a coat and tie the Friday before a game to signify that they are a class act and that their game is an important event. I know of one college team that has a tradition that dates back over 30 years where they eat a tasty pecan roll at their team dinner the night before a game. Prior to home games this same team goes to hear the marching band play fight songs in the gymnasium. Then they walk to the stadium listening to the encouraging cheers of their fans. After each victory they stand before the band and sing their alma mater. These are all very powerful rituals.

Hopefully you already have established rituals for yourself and your team, but if you need assistance then use the exercise below. To develop effective rituals, remember a time when you performed really well and ask yourself what all of your senses were experiencing. **You may also want to develop brand new rituals as a signal that you are leaving the past behind and this is a new season, a new attitude and a new improved you. From this point on things are going to get better.** If you have had rituals in the past that have led to undesirable performance, then stop using those and switch to something new. The key to rituals is that they not only are consistent but that they bring back memories of good performance.

To develop an effective ritual, first think of a positive athletic experience in the past. Then remember and write down what you were tasting, smelling, hearing, seeing, touching and what you were wearing. If you prefer to start fresh, develop creative new ideas for the future:

Taste _____

Smell _____

Sound _____

Sight _____

Touch _____

Clothes _____

The following is an example to help spark some ideas.

Taste: Chew your favorite gum.
Smell & Touch: Massage your calves with muscle ointment.
Sound: Listen to your favorite upbeat song.
Sight: Look at a photograph that inspires you.
Touch: Clap your hands three times.
Clothes: Wear a wrist band that is your team color.

It doesn't matter what your rituals are. What matters is that you have them. Just remember the four keys to having effective rituals:

Rituals

1.) They must spark memories of good performance in the past or confidence for good performance in the future.

2.) They must be consistent.

3.) They should involve your senses and what you wear.

4.) They must be pleasing, exciting and/or inspiring.

~~~~~~

I will close this chapter with a memory that I have of the power of rituals:

I was coaching my daughter's basketball team when she was a senior in high school and we ended the regular season without one victory. Before the tournament started I told the team that everything had been practice up to this point and that we were now ready to play our best in the tournament. To signify this new attitude I told them we were changing our team name. Our team would no longer be called Liberty, but instead from this point on our new name would be "Pizzazz". We would constantly remind ourselves of our new team and our new way of playing with spectacular energy. Our ritual would be to get in a circle and put our hands together in the middle. Then on the count of three we would shout "Pizzazz". We would do this ritual before the game and before we went on the floor after a time out and after half time. This ritual created a completely new identity for our team. After winning the first game of the tournament against the team with the best record, the girls came to every game with "Pizzazz" written on their warm up shirts. They played with confidence and intensity yet they were relaxed and having fun. Every time before going on to the floor they put their hands together, shouted, "Pizzazz", smiled and then went out and played with pizzazz. They went on to win every game and become the tournament champions wowing everyone with their new found enthusiasm and energy. It was a great way to finish the season, but it was an even greater lesson on the power of rituals.

Chapter Eight

<u>Rewards</u>

After every victory our State Championship football coach would encourage us to spend the weekend enjoying our success. We would come back on Monday and start working hard for the next game, but for that weekend our assignment was to reward ourselves and "savor the victory". He understood the power of rewards.

You must reward yourself when you accomplish anything positive that moves you closer to your goal. When you first learned to walk, your parent's encouragement and positive reinforcement were the key to your success. When your mind associates pleasure with the activity you are involved in, it will desire more of it. Hopefully you have coaches, parents or friends that reward you in some way with at least a compliment. You should also reward yourself. The best way to do that is to take time early in the season to write down what your favorite rewards might be. If it's later in the season when you read this chapter, do the exercises anyway. It is never too late to decide how to reward yourself.

You should have three columns, one with small rewards that you would like to receive when you accomplish something in practice or during the pre-season. The second column is for medium rewards that are more significant. These rewards are what you would like to get during the regular season when you accomplish something significant at your game, match, meet or event. The third column is for big rewards that you would like to receive in either post season play or when you achieve your personal goal for the season.

Step 1. Write down your personal goal for the season
(See Chapter 1)

_____
_____
_____
_____

Step 2. List the small, medium and big rewards you would like to receive as you accomplish objectives that will move you closer to your goal. The table below will guide you through the process:

Small Rewards for practices & pre-season	Medium Rewards for the regular season	Big Rewards for post regular season or when goal is achieved

The following are three examples to help you get started.

A.) Athlete: NFL defensive end

Goal: During the 2007 NFL season for the Dallas Cowboys, I had a minimum of 10 quarterback sacks, was voted most valuable defensive lineman, remained completely strong and healthy and totally enjoyed the season.

Rewards that he would like to have as he progresses toward his goal and when he achieves his goal:

Small Rewards for practices & pre-season	Medium Rewards for the regular season	Big Rewards for post regular season or when goal is achieved
Compliment from head coach	Game ball	Huge Bonus
Compliment from the owner	Team sings my college's fight song	My Defensive Line Coach shaves his head

B.) Athlete: High School female basketball player

Goal: During the 2007-2008 basketball season for the Hanover Gales, I was voted Most Improved Player by my teammates and totally enjoyed the season.

Rewards that she would like to have as she progresses toward her goal and when she achieves her goal:

Small Rewards for practices & pre-season	Medium Rewards for the regular season	Big Rewards for post regular season or when goal is achieved
My coach praises me	Shopping	Ipod
Favorite ice cream	Favorite Restaurant	New Clothes & Shoes

C.) Athlete: 7 year old male soccer player

Goal: During the 2007 fall soccer season for the Timpton Rage, I scored a minimum of 10 goals and had fun playing.

Rewards that he would like to have as he progresses toward his goal and when he achieves his goal:

Small Rewards for practices & pre-season	Medium Rewards for the regular season	Big Rewards for post regular season or when goal is achieved
My Coach says "Good Job"	Dairy Queen	Pizza party
Favorite Candy	Movie	Sleepover

For your reward system to be effective you should sit down with your coach and other people that will be involved and let them know what your goals are (see chapter 1). Then agree on what you would like for rewards along the way and when you achieve your goal.

A note to coaches and parents about rewards:

Rewards chosen by the athletes will be much more effective than those chosen by the coach or parent. Only athletes know what will motivate them and make them feel rewarded for their accomplishments. The coach or parent may offer ideas and set limits, but ultimately the rewards need to be chosen by the athletes for maximum effectiveness.

Chapter Nine

<u>Wow</u>

One of the interesting things you need to be prepared for is how to handle your reaction when you start to perform well. This may be new territory for you so it may feel different. "Different" isn't something your mind enjoys. The brain prefers certainty and familiarity. When you achieve success you may experience what I term *"The Wow Phenomenon"* and you must know how to handle this "new you". Unknowingly parents, coaches, fans, the media and even you can really make this a struggle. Statements may be made such as, "You played way over your head", or "You were really in a zone". These types of phrases suggest that your excellent performance was not expected from you. They may cause doubt to emerge in your mind which causes you to retreat to where you were before.

"The Wow Phenomenon" happens to athletes at every level. It can happen for a while during an event or possibly for the entire event. It could even happen for an entire season or multiple seasons. Basketball, baseball and golf are the three sports that come to mind first when I think of *"The Wow Phenomenon"*. Have you ever seen a basketball player or the whole team start "shooting the lights out"? They go on a run where every shot goes in and they score fifteen points before the other team gets any. How about a baseball pitcher that pitches a no hitter or a batter that gets on base

five times in a row? Then there is the golfer that gets a string of birdies.

I am convinced that the reason these experiences occur is because the athletes are allowing themselves to play up to their full potential. Instead of this being an unusual event in the athlete's career it should be viewed as a glimpse of what the athlete is capable of. If athletes have done a lot of mental training, they should not be surprised when their performance is top notch. They have already visualized this level of excellence over and over in their mind, so why be amazed if this type of performance shows up in reality. The best way to handle *"The Wow Phenomenon"* is to simply accept this type of performance as normal behavior.

Another way to handle *"The Wow Phenomenon"* is to go on hyper alert after your excellent performance. If there is any way to shield yourself from the surprised people in your life, then do so. You might choose to not read any articles about yourself. You might politely ask any well-wishers to please not make a big deal out of it. Most importantly control what you know you can control which is primarily your own thoughts. Constantly check the voices. Are they saying doubt-inducing things such as "That was lucky" or "That will never happen again"? If so use the tools in Chapter 4 to wash these types of voices away. Replace them immediately with affirming voices such as, "That was just how I envisioned it" or "That was so much fun, I can't wait to do that again!"

After you have an excellent performance, it is very important to take some time to remember everything about it. Pay attention to what all of your senses were experiencing. What was your body posture and what were you seeing, hearing, tasting, smelling and feeling? This will come in very handy when you do the first two exercises in Chapter 16 that teach you how to raise your spirit prior to competition.

Chapter Ten

<u>Monsters</u>

To be most effective, this chapter along with Chapter 11 and 12 should all be read together at one sitting. Chapter 10 will help you identify what may be holding you back from performing up to your fullest potential. It will also prepare you for the exercise in Chapter 11. Chapter 11 and 12 will provide tools for releasing your fears and enhancing your performance.

At some point in a season, it is common for some athletes to start under-performing. The most common term for this occurrence is a slump. In baseball a player may be hitting well all season and then for some reason he can't hit anything. Although a slump is accepted as normal in baseball, it can happen to anyone in any sport. When I talk to athletes in this situation the first thing I ask is, "What are the monsters?"

Most people don't need any more explanation of what I am asking. They quickly start pouring out all of their fears. The problem becomes very clear, very quickly. Their mind is linking emotional pain with their sport. Therefore, their brain will do its best to protect the athlete from this pain. This protection usually comes in the form of hindering the athlete from participating freely.

If you find yourself under performing, the important thing to realize is that there is nothing wrong with you and that your mind is functioning perfectly. You are not the problem, your brain is not the problem, and you are not a "head case". Your mind is perfectly healthy and is doing exactly what it is designed to do and that is to help you avoid pain. **Know that you possess all the right ingredients to overcome your fears and reach your full potential...a creative imagination and a healthy mind.**

Before teaching you methods to get yourself back on track you must first be taught something that I learned when I was in graduate school. I took an advertising class and wrote a paper on a concept called *"The Pleasure Principle"*. Many effective advertisements are created based on this principle. Simply put, advertisers want to associate the company's product or service with something that your mind thinks is pleasurable.

Let's say that you have just developed a drink product and you want to sell it to as many people as possible. You know the product tastes good, but you also know that it has no healthy benefit because it has a high amount of sugar and caffeine. You have another problem and that is that the color of your drink is black and doesn't look like something people would want to rush out and pour into their bodies. How do you successfully market something like this? It's simple. Use *"The Pleasure Principle"*. Start by packaging your drink with attractive warm feeling colors such as red or blue. Then start an advertising campaign so when people see your drink they associate it with something pleasurable. One idea is to make your commercials humorous so that people will smile and laugh while thinking of your product. Another idea is to show a beautiful woman or handsome man drinking your drink. If they are famous people it would be even more effective. In your commercial show a beautiful nature scene like a mountain range or a beautiful beach while displaying your drink. Come up with a slogan that suggests that your drink is the key to happiness. If you do all of this, then it won't matter what your drink looks like or even what you call it. It will be purchased by millions of people because you have done an excellent job of linking your drink to something pleasurable in the minds of your target market. You have achieved the secret formula for success:

Your drink = Pleasure

Super Bowl commercials cost companies millions of dollars for 60 seconds of exposure. The following are some of the highest rated Super Bowl commercials. As you review these, consider how *"The Pleasure Principle"* was being used:

1995 Pepsi – A little boy on a beach was drinking Pepsi out of a bottle with a straw and loved it so much he kept sucking relentlessly to get the last little drop out. Then suddenly he sucks himself right through the straw and into the bottle. His little sister comes up, looks at him inside the bottle and yells, "Mom, he did it again!"

> The message:
> Pepsi tastes incredibly good.
> Pepsi makes me laugh and feel good.
> Pepsi = Pleasure

1998 Pepsi – When a guy jumps out of a plane to do some sky surfing, a goose flies up and they challenge each other with one-on-one stunts in the air, then they share a can of Pepsi.

The message:
> Pepsi is very exciting.
> Pepsi makes me laugh and feel good.
> Pepsi = Pleasure

2005 Bud Light – A Para trooping instructor is trying to convince his student to jump out of the plane. When the guy won't go he finally throws out a six-pack of Bud Light to entice him to jump. He still doesn't go, but to everyone's surprise the pilot runs up and jumps out after the Bud Light.

The message:
> Bud Light is so good it is worth jumping out of a plane for.
> Bud Light makes me laugh and feel good.
> Bud Light = Pleasure

If companies pay millions of dollars to associate their product with pleasure why don't you take this same information and apply *"The Pleasure Principle"* to your sport? That is what I will now teach you to do.

In the rest of this chapter and the next two chapters, I want you to fully participate because these chapters are designed to get you out of your slump as quick as possible. This isn't something you can do while you are driving. You must be alone in a quiet place and have a pen and a piece of paper. You should not feel rushed. Allow about an hour to get through this three chapter session. If it takes less time for you that's great, but the important thing is that you relax and have plenty of time to finish.

I'm going to give you a couple of examples of sessions I have had with athletes and again I would encourage you to actually participate in all of the exercises that follow.

The first case is about a girl named Lauren who was a State Champion in the 1600 meters her sophomore year. In the Cross Country season of her junior year she was struggling and way under performing. She did not have any physical problems so there was probably something going on inside her head. The night before the District meet, I helped with her mental preparation. She went out the next day, ran her best time, placed second, but most importantly really enjoyed racing again. Here is the process I took her through and if you follow this process using your own situation, you could be impacted just as quickly. Take it seriously, but relax, be as creative as you can be and have fun with this.

Monsters

What are the monsters? Write down all of your fears concerning your sport. What are your thoughts while you are warming up. What about when you are doing your sport? What about when you finish? Who are you afraid of? It is very important that you are totally open and honest with yourself. I would encourage you to write this list in private where no one else can see it. Take some time to write these things down now, then come back and read about the monsters that Lauren was dealing with. Her monsters may help you remember some of your own monsters. If so then add those to your list. Take a moment now to start your list on the next page.

My Monsters:

_____

_____

_____

_____

_____

_____

_____

_____

_____

_____

_____

_____

_____

_____

_____

_____

_____

The biggest monster that Lauren had was the fear of disappointing people if she didn't do well. I call this *"Champions Disease"*. Sometimes after doing well one season, it can become a curse the next season. She had a long list of people that she thought she might disappoint if she didn't perform well. Her parents, her coaches, her teammates, the principal, the janitor, people in college who were on the team last year, her friends, the newspaper reporter...basically anyone who knew her. Can you imagine how much this monster weighed? No wonder she couldn't run fast with this 400 pound creature on her back. How could racing be fun when the main thought was who you were going to disappoint if you didn't do well?

She also imagined that people hated her because of her success last season. She felt as if coaches from other teams, her competitors and parents of her competitors were all watching her with hate in their eyes and wanted her to fail. Now the monster weighs 500 pounds.

She said that before the race she felt like her stomach was hard and tense and her main thought was, "Let's get this over with". Then during the race she would have thoughts such as, "I hate this", "There's that coach that wants me to fall down", "Oh no, there's Mom & Dad, they are going to be so disappointed", "My legs feel so heavy" and "I am never going to do this in college!" Now the monster weighs 600 pounds. After the race she would feel awful and her main thought was, "Thank goodness that's over with."

Hopefully by viewing Lauren's monsters you were able to more easily identify and list your own. The next step is to think of your favorite things.

Favorite Things

After identifying your monsters, remember your favorite things and write them down. In the musical, *The Sound of Music*, there is a song that reminds us that the remedy for feeling bad is to simply remember our favorite things. That is excellent advice. Your next step is to write down your favorite things. What is your favorite upbeat song, your favorite color, animal, place, car, vacation, person, thing that makes you laugh, funny TV character, funny character from a movie, cartoon character, or Disney character? What is your favorite flower, bird, pet, type of butterfly, weather, season, nature scene, holiday, type of clown, taste, smell, sound, anything or anyone that makes you feel good? Stop reading and start writing down your favorite things.

My Favorite Things

_____
_____
_____
_____
_____
_____
_____
_____
_____
_____
_____
_____
_____
_____
_____
_____
_____
_____
_____
_____

Lauren, the girl mentioned earlier, said that her favorite upbeat song at that time was Mombo #5, her favorite color was blue, her favorite animal was a golden retriever, she loved clowns and sunshine, the taste of hot chocolate and the smell of Irish Spring soap. Now we are ready to go to the next exercise which is in the next chapter.

Chapter Eleven

<u>Rewind</u>

This exercise and the next one in Chapter 12 that is called *Slingshot* I learned from Anthony Robbins who is one of the world's most renowned life enhancement coaches. For information on his books, tapes and intense multi-day seminars go to www.anthonyrobbins.com. These exercises are designed to quickly free yourself of monsters and enhance your performance. They are simple and only require your imagination. I've seen these techniques work very effectively with many athletes. It should be noted that these exercises work for entire sporting events or for specific skills such as hitting a baseball, kicking field goals, hitting a golf ball, shooting free throws, hitting a tennis ball, shooting arrows, diving, doing handoff exchanges in a track relay, pole vaulting, catching a football, bowling, etc.

Rewind **is designed to erase the monsters and replace them with power boosters.** As was said in Chapter 10 if you are in a slump it is probably because you have associated emotional pain with your sport. When your brain thinks of your sport it cringes. It doesn't want you to do your sport because you have trained it to believe the following formula: Your sport = emotional pain. It will do what it is supposed to do; it will try to protect you by hindering you from participating.

As quickly as possible we need to erase the old formula that your mind is using and replace it with the success formula: **your sport = sky high pleasure**. That is what *Rewind* is all about. To get you familiar with this exercise I will take you through the process that I went through with Lauren, the girl I talked about in the last chapter.

With her eyes closed I asked her to see in her mind her worst race so far that season. We called it, "The monster race". I asked her to remember what she was thinking, feeling and seeing before the race, during the race and after the race. When she was finished I asked her to rewind the tape of the scenes that she played in her mind. This rewind process took less than 15 seconds. Now we were ready for the fun part. In fact we labeled this next version, "The fun race".

I had her run the same race in her mind but this time we were going to be imaginative and create the most outrageously fun race of all time. I encouraged her to only focus on having fun. It was party time.

As I guided her through the fun race, I interjected images of all of her favorite things. I had her see a blue sky and feel warm sunshine on her face. At different points in the race she saw clowns and golden retrievers. She smelled Irish Spring soap and tasted hot chocolate. She saw her parents and coaches laughing. Her legs felt light and strong. All the while her favorite song was playing and she floated along feeling full of energy and vitality. She kept thinking how much fun this was and how she couldn't wait to see what was up ahead.

After the fun race was over, she rewound very quickly and then started the monster race. After she rewound the monster race, she went back to the fun race. I kept having her alternate the two types of races and rewinding them over and over again. Each monster race became progressively shorter and less vivid. Each fun race became a little longer and more exciting. Finally I noticed that when she was playing the monster race video she was no longer frowning. That was my queue to end the exercise by having her do one more fun race. The monster race had been erased and replaced with the fun race. Now when she thought of racing she thought of a pleasing and positive experience. For her this took about 10 rewinds of each race and that is what I have found to be the approximate number it takes to be effective.

This *Rewind* technique can be effective by yourself or you can have someone help guide you through your video. If you have help make sure that the person is imaginative so they can help ignite your creativity.

Let's review the three step process:

1.) Identify your monsters
2.) Identify your favorite things
3.) Do the *Rewind* exercise

First review the list of your monsters that you identified. Now close your eyes and run the monster video of your sporting event. Throw in as many of the monsters as you can and feel all of the pain during the entire event from start to finish. Then rewind within about 15 seconds.

Now look at your list of favorite things. Then close your eyes and start your fun video. Remember results don't matter. What about the location, is it your favorite nature scene? Are you on a mountain, in a forest, or on a beach? Be creative as you add your favorite upbeat song. Feel your spirits rise as you get into the rhythm of the music. Add your favorite color and your favorite smell. Feel how they give you energy. Make the day your favorite kind of weather and feel how great that makes you feel. Laugh at one of the things that used to be a monster, but now it looks like something funny. Keep doing your sport and feel how much energy you have and how much fun you are having. Keep hearing the music. Smile as you see your favorite animal. Is it flying? Is it dancing? Are you riding it? See something that gets you excited as you approach the end of the video. Go celebrate by doing something outrageous. How about running through a huge waterfall? When you are done then rewind within about 15 seconds.

When you are back at the beginning, shift gears and replay the monster video again. When finished with that, rewind it very quickly within about 8 seconds. Then replay the fun video adding even more treats to your collection of favorite things and feeling how great this video makes you feel. Then rewind it again but this time even quicker. Go through the same process again and again for at least 10 times. Always finish with the fun video.

~~~~~

A vivid display of the impact of *Rewind* was demonstrated in the 2005 NCAA Basketball Championships. Michigan State made it to the tournament, but had lost to Iowa in the Big Ten Championship. Before the NCAA tournament started, the coach, Tom Izzo, had his players watch a video of their loss to Iowa. Then he pulled the tape out, threw it on the floor and smashed it with a big sledge hammer. That got everyone's attention about how serious he was about forgetting past mistakes. Then he put in a highlight video of all of the great plays they had made that season. What a great coaching strategy. Erasing past mistakes and replacing them with images of best performances is a powerful tool. Michigan State who was seeded sixth in their region went on to defeat higher ranked teams and made it into the Final Four.

Chapter Twelve

<u>Slingshot</u>

This exercise is a very quick way to replace negative images with positive images. If your imagination has associated your sport with emotional pain, *Slingshot* is another effective tool to help you get back on track and reach your full potential. This exercise can be used by itself or it can be used right after *Rewind* to strengthen you even further.

Step 1

Keep your eyes open and see a large picture frame in front of you. This frame should be at least 2 feet across and 3 feet from top to bottom. In this frame see the ugly picture of your last disappointing performance. Feel the pain and frustration that it caused you. Now behind that picture see a small picture frame about six inches wide and eight inches tall. In that frame create a beautiful picture of your greatest moment in your sport. Experience how awesome that moment made you feel. See that this small frame is about three feet behind the large frame and is attached to the large frame with rubber bands like a slingshot.

Step 2

In a moment you will pull the small picture back, stretching those rubber bands. Then you will let it go and watch it become as big as the other picture as it slams into it and completely destroys it. When it hits the other picture you need to shout a one syllable word that describes the crashing sound. Something like "Bam" or "Boom" will do. You must shout this word right when you see the positive picture crash into the ugly picture. You are going to do this at least 12 times in a row and do it very quickly. On the last one, when the positive picture hits the ugly picture, destroy the ugly picture, replace it with the positive one and hold it in your mind for about ten seconds.

After *Rewind* and *Slingshot* the next step is to get focused with a quick three step goal setting session. Think about your upcoming event. What is your goal, the reasons it is important to you, and what action is necessary. Lauren, the Cross Country runner, wrote down the following:

Goal: On October 24, 1998 in the High School Cross Country District Championship, I ran my best time of the year, qualified for Regionals, and totally enjoyed the race.

Why: Because I love to run. Because I love to compete. Because I will advance to Regionals and have the opportunity to run again. Because it is the most incredibly awesome feeling to do my best. Because I am so excited about making a statement to everyone that I am back.

Action: Visualize my Fun Race before I go to sleep tonight and again the first thing when I wake up tomorrow. Eat a good breakfast. Be friendly, but stay away from idle conversations or other distractions. Know that I AM a focused, confident, & powerful athlete. Listen to my favorite song. Stand guard and laugh away any negative thoughts. Warm up 40 minutes before the race. Get to the starting line 5 minutes ahead. Run like the wind.

After you complete your Goal, Why and Action statements (see Chapter 1), you should adopt some of the above action steps so you are totally prepared. Definitely visualize your fun event before you go to sleep and right when you wake up. Claim your "I AM" statement (read Chapter 2 again if necessary). Listen to your favorite upbeat song & laugh away any negative voices.

What you have accomplished in the last three chapters 10 through 12 is to learn how to use the incredible power of *"The Pleasure Principle"* to convince yourself that participating in your sport is a very enjoyable thing to do.

The following is a review of the process:

1.) Identify your monsters
2.) Identify your favorite things
3.) Do the *Rewind* exercise
4.) Do the *Slingshot* exercise
5.) Do the three step Goal Setting exercise
6.) Take appropriate action

If you follow these steps you will break out of a slump quickly and be back on your way to performing at your peak level.

~~~~~

The rest of the story about Lauren:

Remember the thoughts Lauren had about racing that were revealed on page 67? She said at the time she hated to run and that she would never run in college. As it turned out she received a track and cross country scholarship to Penn State University and ran all four years. After college she started competing in triathlons and marathons. As of this writing she has run in eight marathons.

Chapter Thirteen

Panic

Imagine this situation. You feel like you have prepared well both physically and mentally for your competition and have a sense of confidence every day prior to and including the day of the event. But as the actual starting time approaches, you feel like you are losing your confidence. This feeling is more than a healthy case of nervousness. You are overcome with fear. You become disoriented and feel completely weak. You may even have trouble breathing and feel like you are choking. If you don't have an action plan to deal with this feeling of panic, you probably will "choke" when you attempt to perform.

Here is the key distinction about panic: it is not a weak personality trait that you were born with and cannot overcome. Panic is simply caused by the athlete's *interpretation* of the situation. When you are up against stiff competition you can react in one of two ways: panic or excitement. Panic is based on fear whereas excitement is based on joy. The difference is all about how your mind is interpreting the pressure. One athlete might thrive on this type of pressure and become excited about it much like a young child on Christmas morning. Perfect examples are the basketball players like Michael Jordan or LeBron James that want to take the last shot in a close double overtime game. Football quarterbacks like Tom Brady or Peyton Manning who thrive on leading their teams to come from behind victories. Runners like Steve Prefontaine that loved to hold off a challenger in the home stretch. Golfers like Jack Nicklaus and Tiger Woods who love to compete in a playoff. These types of athletes truly enjoy every aspect of their sport, but especially the toughest situations against the toughest competition. They have chosen to interpret these experiences as very special and exciting. The athletes who feel panic and experience "choking" have chosen to interpret the pressure of their situation as something to be afraid of.

To illustrate my point, I'll use an example of a roller coaster ride. At Cedar Point in Sandusky, Ohio there are many coasters one of which is called The Millennium Force. This wild ride takes you up higher than any coaster in the world and then it plummets almost straight down. It continues to romp around its track at speeds over 90 MPH. Some people love this coaster and find it to be an exhilarating experience. Others get scared out of their minds. After they are scraped out of their seats at the end of the ride they never want to be seen near that coaster again. It's the same roller coaster, but two completely different interpretations of the experience. **The good news is that interpretations can change, which means that panic can be overcome.**

When panic hits, it is usually best to have a coach or teammate help you implement a quick panic relief strategy. However, you could do these exercises by yourself.

1.) *Slingshot* – See Chapter 12. This is a fast acting way to turn your thoughts away from fear and get refocused and confident again.

I will never forget this one track athlete that came up to me 15 minutes before she had to run an 800 meter run. She told me she had run her worst time ever on the 4X800 relay earlier that day, so she was completely fearful about running another bad race again. I knew I didn't have a lot of time, so I led her through the *Slingshot* exercise which only takes about a minute. After her race she came up to me with a big smile on her face and said she ran her best time ever! This technique worked well for her because she had worked hard all season and was physically prepared to perform. She just needed a quick technique to help her replace the bad memory of her first race with a remembrance of her best race.

2.) **Goal** – See Chapter 1. Sometimes when you are in a state of panic it is helpful to take a moment and remind yourself of your goal for that event. Say out loud to someone or yourself what your goal is today. State it in terms as if it has already happened. This will help stop all of the thoughts that are spinning around in your head and will get you focused on what you are really up to. Then say out loud why you are accomplishing your goal and describe it in illustrious terms. This will help ignite passion for your mission and will replace those fearful emotions. Finally, get focused by reviewing your strategy. Now you know what you intend to do, why you intend to do it, and how you are going to make it happen. You are back on track.

3.) **Laugh** – See Chapter 4. After doing #1 and #2 above, stand guard at the door of your mind until your competition starts. Do this during your event as well and discard any negative thoughts by laughing at them.

If you are unable to get over the fear and you end up "choking", focus on learning from the experience and realizing that it doesn't have to be the same the next time. The more you are faced with a fear-inducing type of situation, the better you will be able to handle it in the future. Experience, maturity and patience are great teachers. If you need more help, review all the chapters of this book, but especially chapters 3, 4, 10, 11, and 12.

Chapter Fourteen

<u>Oops</u>

This chapter is extremely important because it provides tools to use when you don't achieve your objective. At some point in time every athlete makes a mistake or experiences a loss. It may be a small mistake or big mistake. It may be a loss during the regular season or it may be losing a major championship. Whether the *"Oops"* is big or small, you better know how to deal with it.

I think all athletes, but especially precision athletes such as divers, field goal kickers and archers, can learn about handling mistakes from the best professional golfers. These athletes are at the top consistently because they have mastered this mental skill of quickly overcoming their mistakes.

I will never forget watching Jack Nicklaus play in The Memorial Tournament one year when he was two strokes in the lead with two holes to go. To everyone's surprise he sliced his tee shot and it ended up on the deck of someone's home along side the 17th fairway. Many people would have folded at that point, but Jack thought differently. He took a penalty stroke and hit a beautiful drive. He then hit an approach shot that was close enough to knock in for a bogey. His competitor had a par so Jack was only up by one stroke going into the final hole. His tee shot went into the fairway bunker on the right. His second shot went into the deep trap left of the green. His challenger was down the middle on his drive and just off the green on his second shot.

Imagine what Jack Nicklaus was thinking. Do you think he was calling himself derogatory names? Do you think he was asking himself ridiculing questions? Do you think he started visualizing his interview with the T.V. announcers explaining how he blew up on the last two holes of his own golf course to lose his own tournament? Do you think he thought about the people he was going to disappoint? The actions he took confirmed that his thoughts remained focused, confident and competitive. He hit his third shot out of the sand and landed it three feet from the pin. His competitor had a nice chip and putt for a par. Jack had to make his putt for the win, which he did because he knew how to handle the *"Oops"*.

The following are some tools that can help you effectively handle the *"Oops"*:

1.) **Express-less**

If you don't perform well, then let's face it, you are going to feel disappointed, angry and hurt. That's normal, but what you need to understand is that **the stronger your emotion is about your undesirable performance, the easier it will be to recall. To prevent that from happening you will need to minimize your reaction to it.** So be careful with your emotions.

Another important word about expressing disappointment is to never allow any form of expression to be demeaning to you or another person. Dumping hurtful garbage on people only makes matters worse.

2.) Questions

Consider the following situations:

> A golfer misses a two foot putt.
> A field goal kicker misses a 10 yard attempt.
> A soccer or hockey goalie allows 4 goals.
> A long jumper fouls on all three attempts.
> A basketball player misses a lay up.
> A baseball shortstop fumbles a ground ball.

What are the questions that the athlete could come up with? How about, "How could I be so bad?" If you ask that question then your mind would start looking for answers. Probably other mistakes you've made in the past would come to mind. You have reinforced the negative thought and started a downward spiral that will hurt your performance.

What about if you were just as frustrated and angry after the mistake was made but the first question that entered your head was, "How can I do this better?" or "What can I do next time to make sure this doesn't happen again." Then your mind starts searching for answers and suddenly new insights come in. **Be very careful about the questions you find yourself asking. If they are demeaning, quickly erase them by changing the questions to something helpful.**

3.) Avoid *"Analysis Paralysis"*

The natural reaction to making a mistake is to start analyzing what went wrong. This scrutiny becomes counter productive if done during competition because the athlete thinks too much about his form or mechanics. For example, if a golfer has a bad shot during a tournament he may start analyzing every phase of his swing. Then his next shot is even worse. **A perfect term for this phenomenon is** *"Analysis Paralysis".* **It means that you are simply thinking too much. When you are performing it is time to be fluid, smooth and without thoughts of your mechanics.** Practice is the time and place for analyzing.

4.) Get Up

One of the most valuable lessons I learned playing sports came after losing a championship football game my sophomore year. Our coach quoted a poem that was written about a soldier after a battle who said something like, *"I guess I'll lie down and cry awhile and then I'll get up and fight again."* Our coach was a great teacher and he seized this opportunity to teach us that life would be filled with disappointments but to always get back up and fight again.

5.) Review

A.) *Thoughts* – Take out a pad of paper, draw two columns labeled "up" and "down" and write down what your inner comments and questions and images were before and during your event. If you have a lot of weak or demeaning thoughts in the "down" column I suggest you go to Chapter 4 on "Voices" and implement the exercises given there. I encourage you to use the exercises called *"Rewind"* and *"Slingshot"* in Chapter 11 and 12 to help erase this memory and restore your confidence.

B.) *Now* – Ask yourself if during your athletic event you were staying focused on the present moment or if you were thinking about anything else such as previous events, future events or future rewards. See Chapter 5 for help.

C.) **Strategy** – A critical review of your strategy should be encouraged by you and your coach. Constructive criticism that focuses on how your strategy could be more effective should always be viewed as helpful.

D.) **Preparation** – Ask yourself and ask your coach how you could be better prepared both physically and mentally for the next competition.

6.) **Victimless**

Avoid developing feelings of being a victim. If you find yourself blaming others - like the referees, the other coaches, the fans or your own teammates, you are probably feeling like a victim. The time to stop thinking like a victim is now because these types of thoughts are very unhealthy and unproductive. **The most productive thoughts you can have are to stop blaming others and accept responsibility for your results. Then and only then can you take charge of improving your performance.**

7.) **Perception**

When you lose, make a mistake or don't perform well, it is helpful to consider that situation from a positive perspective. The following are a few thoughts to consider:

Just getting warmed up. This attitude works well if mistakes are made early in a competition. Instead of getting into a downward spiral of negative thoughts, simply adopt the attitude that you are "just getting warmed up". **This thought confirms your confidence. It reminds you that making a few mistakes is just part of the game and that you will get back on track soon.**

You aren't what you accomplish. **You should never confuse your accomplishments or your lack of accomplishments with your value as a human being.** If you don't perform well or accomplish your goals that situation may make you feel disappointed, but it certainly does not make you a failure.

Turning Point. This negative experience could be the point at which everything changes for you. You see this in sports all of the time. You see this in life all of the time. When things look bleak the momentum shifts and things keep getting better from that point on. This occurs when **the athletes decide then and there that it's going to be different from that point on and nothing is going to stop them.** At a graduation ceremony I heard the valedictorian quote someone who said, **"What is more important than how high you reach when you are successful, is how high you bounce when you hit bottom."**

Next Play. The center on our high school football team, who is now a surgeon, told me about an important lesson he taught his kids when they were playing sports. "Don't dwell on the last mistake but move on and do better next time." To help them easily remember this lesson he called it, "Next Play". Later in life he was involved in a lawsuit and lost the case. Initially he was shocked at the unfairness of the judge's decision, but one of his sons tapped him on the shoulder and whispered, "Next Play." He realized he had to not let it get him down, learn from it, and move on. The next play has nothing to do with the last play. **Leave the last play and all the negative emotions behind. It is time to start fresh with no extra baggage weighing you down. The next play is a new play.**

Precision athletes such as golfers and baseball pitchers really have to keep this concept in mind because mistakes are so likely to happen during the course of their games. For the golfer, "Next Shot" or "Next Hole" and for the pitcher, "Next Pitch", "Next Batter" or "Next Inning" would be effective phrases to adopt. These words will keep the inevitable mistakes from multiplying and ruining the entire game.

There is no failure, only lessons. When things don't work out as you had hoped, ask yourself what beneficial things you learned from the experience. You will begin to realize that **every outcome is just an opportunity to learn and improve.**

I believe the most disappointing occurrence is when an athlete suffers a season-ending injury. Instead of dwelling on the disappointment surrounding this situation, it is extremely beneficial to search for the lessons. I will never forget a very talented runner named Jill. She had exceptional performance her junior track season and was expected to place in the top two in the State her senior year. However, a mysterious foot injury ruined her entire senior season. Even with X-Rays, MRI's and bone scans no medical professional could clearly identify the source of her pain. She trained in the pool every day hoping that her foot would heal enough so that she could run in the final meets of the year. She attempted to run in The District Meet but the pain made her stop on the first curve. Her dream was crushed.

It is important to grieve for awhile after something like this happens. Then it becomes important to look for the lessons. Sometimes the lessons are very clear and other times they are not clear for years to come. Sometimes they are very simple lessons and sometimes they are so profound that they can make a life changing type of impact. So attempts at defining the lessons are just guesses, but that is better than sitting around feeling awful.

In Jill's case we considered many possible lessons. I will share them with you in hopes that you may find something that applies to your situation:

Diet - To learn more about what your body needs to maintain strong bones and muscles.

Training - To train less on hard surfaces and more on soft surfaces.

Body Balance - To get your body more in balance so that all the load bearing joints carry the weight they were designed to carry.

Sleep - To get more sleep so the body can produce more and repair more.

Life Balance - To be careful not to be so driven about achieving your goal, that you ignore other important parts of your life such as your health.

Rhythm - It is important to work hard, but you must also spend time relaxing. Watch a wave and see how it hits the beach, then retreats, gains more power and hits the beach again. It is this rhythm of working hard, then rejuvenating, then working hard again that leads to effective results. Consider those things that help you relax and make them a priority.

Caregivers - To recognize how many people care about you. To know that you have a strong support system of family and friends that are here to love you, nurture you, guide you, assist you, encourage you, laugh with you, cry with you and just be there for you.

Occupation - To realize that modern medicine is far from perfect and that the world needs more health care professionals who can diagnose and heal people with a high degree of effectiveness. You may decide to become one of them.

Empathy - To go through this experience so you can help others that go through similar types of experiences in a compassionate and effective manner.

Impact - To know that even though you didn't compete for your team that you still had a huge impact on your teammates. Because you are a great role model your teammates will compete with the courage, determination, focus and heart of their finest teacher.

The rest of the story about Jill:

The summer before her freshman year in college Jill's foot injury was finally properly diagnosed as a ganglion cyst. The pressure from the cyst had fractured a metatarsal bone. The cyst was drained and her bone healed in time for Cross Country season in the fall.   Jill received a Track and Cross Country scholarship from Wake Forest University and ran all four years. At Wake she became Junior All American, Indoor All American and two-time Academic All American.

When asked seven years later if she had in fact learned anything from that painfully disappointing experience in high school, she responded as follows:

"That experience taught me to have a bigger perspective than just accomplishing my athletic goal. As you go through a season regardless if you meet your objective or not you are still getting better as a person. Each curve ball that is thrown at you is there to teach you and make you a better person. I realized that I got through that ugly time in my life and now I know I can get through other tough times. I learned that while it is important to strive for big goals that you should take time to have fun building relationships with teammates and enjoying every step along the way. Success is measured by what you learned, how you grew stronger, the relationships that you made and the fun that you had."

Chapter Fifteen

<u>Burnout</u>

Many seasons are very long and by the time the last few games, matches, events, or tournaments come around many athletes start to experience burnout. This is more likely to happen if the season has not gone well. **Burnout occurs primarily for two reasons: lack of reward and/or lack of spirit.** The importance of reward is highlighted in Chapter 8 and should be reviewed again if you are feeling burnout or to prevent burnout from happening. If your lack of reward has been the result of many disappointing losses, then a new goal needs to be set for the later part of the season. My suggestion is for you to understand the importance of finishing strong regardless of your record. If questions such as, "What's the use of continuing" start appearing in your mind, the simple answer is, "Because I finish strong." If you find yourself in this position as your season nears an end, go over the exercises in this book and establish a new goal, claim a new identity, develop a new passion for finishing strong and monitor your thoughts. After all, the way you end your season will be what you remember the most and will set the tone for next season. So choose to do your best. Choose to finish strong.

Burnout also commonly occurs because the athlete's spirit has declined. Spirit is like a light bulb that has a dimmer switch. The knob can be turned all the way up which is typically the case at the beginning of a new season, but it can start to dim as a long season nears its end. The dimming process occurs because the athlete didn't take care of his spirit. Most athletes think that they can just keep working hard all season and they will never tire. However, everyone needs to focus on their spirit and develop ways to turn up the dimmer switch.

The next chapter provides twelve ways to ignite your spirit and increase your energy. I encourage you to take this chapter very seriously and to come back to it frequently during your season to keep your light shining brightly.

Chapter Sixteen

<u>Spirit</u>

In order to reach your full potential your spirit must be alive and vibrant. The goal of this chapter is to give you twelve effective tools for lifting your spirit and giving you more energy. You can view this list as a smorgasbord of opportunities for you to sample and decide which ones are most effective for you. The exercise for this chapter is to pick your top three methods from this list. Then implement these techniques for the remainder of the month. At the beginning of the next month come back to this list and choose three more tools to implement that month. Do this each month during your pre-season and regular season.

1. Body

It is true that your emotions have a big impact on the way your body looks, but the opposite is also true...**your body has a huge impact on your emotions.** Try putting a big grin on your face right now. Stand up tall and keep smiling. Now raise your arms in the air as far as they will go and keep smiling. Without changing anything, ask yourself if this makes you feel any better than you did before? Stay in this position and now try feeling sad. It is difficult to do isn't it? That is a small sample of the power your body has over your emotions. Use this to your advantage before your competition. Get your body in a position that will invoke the types of emotions you want to have to perform at your peak. Try it right now.

Let's say that alertness, confidence, & energy are important traits for your sport. So what does your body look like when you are completely alert? What do you look like when you are totally confident? How about when you are really energetic? Get your body in a position that if someone looked at you they would see alertness, confidence and energy. What's your posture look like? What's your face look like? Where are your arms and your hands? How are you standing? If you look alert, confident and energetic you will feel that way as well.

2. Trigger

Start by remembering a time when you were at your peak performance and felt like you were unstoppable. Feel everything about that experience. If possible use all of your senses. See it, taste it, smell it, touch it, hear it. When you are really feeling it, do something physical that will become your trigger for remembering this state of mind again. Some examples are pumping your arm up high, pounding your chest, or clenching your fist. The next time you need to get into this peak state of mind pull your trigger and it should flash back quickly.

A friend brought me some dust from an Olympic Stadium and asked me to use it to motivate the local track team as they went into their most important meets. I decided to use it as a trigger. I had the athletes remember a time when they were at their peak performance while competing in their event. I had them take some of the dust, place it on their chest and pound it with their fist. I gave each of them a canister of the dust to take with them and put on their uniform before each meet. As they prepared to start their event, they would pound their Olympic dust to quickly get into a peak state of mind. Most of them commented afterward that, "It was kind of corny, but it really worked."

3. Music

Music is a key ingredient for lifting your spirit, but not just any music. It must have an upbeat rhythm and if it has words, make sure they are positive. I've heard some songs that have a great beat, but the lyrics contain profanity or a depressing message. Choosing your own songs is the best, but I have included at the end of this book a list of over 135 songs that work well. Many of these songs are "old school", but they are classics and timeless. I was impressed when I heard that Kyle Orton, the quarterback for Purdue University in 2004 listened to *The Doors* before his games. I know a world class sprinter who used to listen to *Earth, Wind & Fire* before every race. The point is that there are inspirational songs from every era and from every genre. Listen to every type of music you can and choose your top ten or twenty pump up songs that work best for you.

In an appropriate situation music can even be used effectively during competition. I will never forget an incident when I was coaching a baseball team. We were in the last inning of the final game of the Championship and were winning 6 – 3. Our pitcher had played a great game and we needed three more outs to win the Championship. After he walked the first three batters, I called a timeout. I walked out to the mound and the only thing I said was, "Sing with me." He smiled and we started singing, "Oh, Happy Day". After about two lines of the song, he smiled and said, "I'm back." Then he went on to strike out the next three batters. All he needed was to get his rhythm back and I know of no better way to do that but through music.

4. Laughter

Laughter is great medicine for your spirit. Don't think for one moment that if you laugh you are not taking your task seriously. Instead realize that the thing that you should be the most serious about is laughter. Laughter is critical to reaching your full potential. A good round of laughter releases chemicals in your body that enhance your sense of well being.

Laughter is a very effective way to break disempowering thought patterns of fear. I remember before a "big" football game I felt very nervous and my performance in warm-ups was horrible. Fortunately, I looked over at our coach and saw him laughing with another coach. That helped me to relax and remember that we weren't on death row, we were out there to play a game and enjoy it.

I will never forget the morning before an important college track meet when I was lying in bed wondering how our relay team could possibly do well against the top schools in the country that were coming to town. I was anxious and was feeling tight all over my body. I was very serious about the task at hand, so serious that I would have probably performed poorly if it had not been for my teammate in the next room. Suddenly I heard a loud noise, something rattling and loud chanting. I walked over to his room and there he was on top of his dresser dancing like a monkey and howling victory chants like, "Can't wait to run today, gonna fly by anybody in my way." I started laughing and my body relaxed, my mind released the fear and I started to feel unstoppable instead of paralyzed. We all ran our best times that day and won the race.

If you want to learn more about the positive impact of laughter, I suggest you study a book called *Anatomy of an Illness* by Norman Cousins. This book (also a movie) tells how this man used laughter as a key element in conquering a life threatening illness. To assure that he had enough laughter in his day, he would watch movies that made him laugh every morning and throughout the day. Because his laughter was disturbing the other patients in the hospital, he moved to an apartment so he could continue his daily medicine of laughter. He took it seriously. So should you.

5. Movies

Inspirational movies should be a steady diet for any athlete looking to enhance performance. Make sure the theme of the movie is uplifting and watch it the night before your competition. On the next page are just a few suggestions of some of the classics:

Movie	Sport
A League of Their Own	Baseball
Coach Carter	Basketball
Cool Runnings	Bob Sledding
Chariots of Fire	Track
Cinderella Man	Boxing
Field of Dreams	Baseball
Friday Night Lights	Football
Heir to a Dream (Pete Maravich)	Basketball
Hoosiers	Basketball
Miracle	Ice Hockey
Rocky	Boxing
Remember the Titans	Football
Rudy	Football
Running Brave (Billy Mills story)	Track
Seabiscuit	Horse Racing
The Natural	Baseball
The Rookie	Baseball
Without Limits (Steve Prefontaine)	Track

One very effective exercise is to watch certain inspirational scenes from movies. I have used this technique before important events and regardless of the sport and regardless of the age of the athletes, it has had a significant positive impact on the spirit of everyone involved. Here are a few examples:

Dead Poets Society – The teacher (Robin Williams) takes the boys in his class out in the hallway and shows them the pictures of previous athletes in the trophy case. Then he says, "Listen real close and you can hear them whisper their legacy to you. Carpe Diem. Seize the day. Make your lives extraordinary."

Spirit

Hoosiers – In the locker room before the Indiana High School State Championship basketball game where the small school was about to play the large school, the coach of the small school asks if anyone has anything to say. One player says, "Let's win this one for all of the small schools that never had a chance to get here." Another player says, "I want to win for my Dad." Another player adds, "Let's win for coach who got us here." The whole game scene is great, but the closing few seconds where the small school wins on a last second shot is classic. I know of a small school that made it to the State basketball tournament and they watched Hoosiers every night of the tournament and ended up winning the Championship.

Rudy – Rudy was a small walk-on on Notre Dame's football team who got beat up in practice everyday for four years, but was never allowed to play in a game. The thrilling scene to watch is the last 20 seconds of their final home game when the crowd starts chanting for Rudy and the coach puts him in for the last kickoff and final play. He sacks the quarterback and the crowd carries him off the field.

Professional Athlete's videos – It is always inspiring to watch people who are excellent at a particular sport. My favorite videos are of Michael Jordan and my favorite scene is the review of Michael playing in the 1992 NBA finals. Michael Jordan was great every time he stepped on the floor, but to see this exceptional athlete in a zone like he was that night was just astonishing. He kept hitting three pointers like they were lay ups. Everything he put up went in.

Rocky – The training scenes of all the Rocky movies are inspiring for any athlete. My favorite is the first Rocky movie. With the song, "Gonna Fly Now" playing in the background Rocky goes through a series of training scenes. Using slabs of meat as punching bags, doing one arm pushups, and running at top speed with a strong finish up the steps of the Philadelphia Art Museum in his black high-top Converse shoes. The scene ends with him raising his arms high in the air celebrating his excellent physical condition, his victory over pain, and displaying his confidence.

~~~~~

During the 2005 NCAA Basketball Tournament, Sean May, the Most Valuable Player of the tournament and center for the University of North Carolina used a movie in a very effective way. His Father had played for Indiana University when they won the Championship in 1976. Sean carried the video of this victory in his bag throughout the entire tournament. The night before the final game he played the video for the team. He wanted his team to see what it looked like to win the National Championship and he wanted to be reminded of what his Dad did to help his team get there. Indiana won in 1976 with Scott May scoring 26 points and getting 8 rebounds. North Carolina won in 2005 with Sean May scoring 26 points and grabbing 9 rebounds.

6. Stillness

Another important key to reviving the spirit is to quiet the mind. **Most athletes only think of revving up the mind, but it is just as important to spend time in stillness.** Find a quiet place, sit in a comfortable chair, take off your shoes, close your eyes and be still. I recommend starting with 10 minutes of stillness a day and building to 15 to 20 minutes every day. Because stillness has a calming effect it should be done no sooner than two hours prior to your workout or competition. The stillness technique is different than the time you spend visualizing, because the purpose of this exercise is to think of nothing. The intent is to give your mind a rest. If you have never done this before, you will most likely have many thoughts the first few times. Be patient with yourself. Sit and relax and don't try. This is one time when you are not to judge or evaluate or label your experience.

If you have tried to have a stillness session for a few days and you feel a need to focus on something to quiet your thoughts, concentrate on the energy that flows through your body. Start with your hands and feel the energy in them. Then feel it in your arms, then your feet, then your legs. Keep going all over your body and feel the energy that is there. Again be patient with yourself and keep guiding your thoughts toward feeling your energy during these stillness sessions. With time the feeling will become stronger.

Another way to make this time more effective is to read something inspirational before you go into stillness. The reading could be just one word. During stillness you could just focus on that one word and repeat it to yourself over and over. Remember the intent here is to quiet the mind not to get pumped up, so choose your word carefully. For example, the word, "peace" or "hope" would be better choices than "strength" or "power".

Yet another method to use during your stillness time is to focus on your breathing. Start by taking a few deep breaths and feel the air coming in through your nose and into your lungs. Then hold it there for a few seconds and slowly let it out. Continue to focus on your breathing as the rate slows to your normal pace. You may want to pick two words to say to yourself as you breathe, one while you inhale and one while you exhale. Choose the words carefully as they need to help quiet the mind. For example, you might say "peace" while inhaling and "calm" while exhaling.

Should you fall asleep during your stillness session that simply means that you needed a short nap and many times that is all you needed to boost your spirit. It also is a clear message that you need more sleep at night.

7. Variety

An effective way to lift your spirit is to get out of your routine and do some physical activity that you really enjoy. Make sure this activity is different than your sport and is safe. An hour long walk is always a good idea. If your sport doesn't involve running then go out for a ten or fifteen minute run. Some other examples are Frisbee golf, throwing an Aerobie, jumping rope, skipping, biking, dancing, swimming, roller blading, flying a kite, jumping on a trampoline, or hula-hooping. Still more ideas are skating, using a punching bag, playing ping pong, foosball, badminton, volleyball, croquet, bocce ball, tennis, racquetball, ultimate Frisbee, you name it. Just do something that is safe, really fun for you and is different than your current sport.

8. Balance

There are many exercises to help your body feel in balance. Being in balance physically tends to heighten your sense of well being. I have learned body balancing techniques from a gentleman named Pete Egoscue who has a clinic in San Diego and is the author of a book entitled *Pain Free*. His website is www.egoscue.com. Pete recommends a series of exercises based on an evaluation of your body posture. Everyone needs different types of exercises, but I have found that a quick way to get my body in balance in less than 10 minutes is to do these two exercises:

A.) Leg Raise – Lie on the floor and put the back of your legs up against a wall so your body forms an L shape. Make sure your bottom is as close to the wall as possible and keep your legs straight and together. Let your arms lie to your sides with your palms facing up. Now relax and hold this position for 4 minutes.

B.) Wall Sit – Sit on the floor with your back against the wall and your legs straight out in front of you. Keep your shoulders and head against the wall and your hands resting comfortably on your thighs. Hold this position for 4 minutes.

9. Shake

Shaking your body enlivens your spirit. If you have ever done the "Hokey Pokey" you know how much fun it is to do that dance and how good everyone feels afterward. Just like in the "Hokey Pokey" you want to shake every body part. I suggest two quick exercises:

A.) Leg Shake – Lie on your back with your legs up in the air and put your hands behind your hips for support. Then shake your legs quickly for 15 seconds. Rest and do it one more time.

B.) Arm & Hand Shake – Stand with your legs firm on the ground about shoulder width apart. Put your arms straight out in front of you and start shaking your hands and arms for about 15 seconds. Then move your arms straight above you and shake again for 15 seconds. Then move your arms out to the sides and shake again for 15 seconds. Finally, move your arms down to your sides and shake for another 15 seconds.

10. Slap

Slapping various areas of your body is another way to ignite your energy. Tarzan knew what he was doing when he would pound on his chest before swinging through the trees.

The most extreme use of this exercise that I have seen is used by a professional football lineman. Right before he goes out of the locker room to play a game he has the trainer slap him in the face. That not only wakes him up, but it also makes him angry which is an emotion that football lineman can use to their advantage.

The less extreme yet very effective method I would recommend is the following. You should be standing for this exercise that lasts a total of about two minutes. Start with your stomach and slap it with both hands at the same time at least 50 and no more than 100 times. This should be done in a rapid and rhythmic fashion. When finished, relax your arms for a moment and then put your hands above your head and start tapping your fingers on the top of your head for about 15 seconds. Then for the next 15 seconds slap your left shoulder and go all the way down the outside of your arm, clap your hands together a few times and then go back up the under side of your arm. Do the same thing on the other shoulder and arm for 15 seconds. Now for the next 15 seconds start at your right buttocks and slap all the way down the back of your leg. Then do the same on your other leg. Now in the last 15 seconds use both hands and slap the middle of your chest starting from the top and going down to your stomach.

11. Quickness

I have found this exercise to be particularly effective if done the day before a competition and as part of a warm up prior to an event. Move different parts of your body quickly to ignite your energy and get your mind focused. The following is an example of how just 60 seconds of quickness can get you going:

1. Run in place with very short steps as quick as your legs will go for 10 seconds.
2. Spread your arms out to your side and swing them in big circles as quickly as you can for 10 seconds then stop and go the other way for another 10 seconds.
3. Do another quickness set with your legs and feet for 10 seconds but this time move around.
4. For 10 seconds quickly swing your arms as if you are sprinting.
5. Clap your hands together as quickly as you can for the final 10 seconds.

12. Stretch

Normally I would think that stretching would be such an obvious pre-event routine that I would not have to mention it. However I've seen too many athletes that de-emphasize stretching and don't understand how it can help lift the spirit. An entire book could be written on stretching, but I will provide eleven exercises as a bare minimum to help athletes get started on a sound stretching program. Please remember to warm up your muscles before stretching. For example, a warm up could be accomplished with a brief 5 or 10 minute jog or bike ride.

A.) *Arms* – Stand tall and clasp your hands together by weaving your fingers together. Turn your hands so that you see the back side of your hands and fingers. Extend your arms in front of you and stretch your hands. Holding that position, now raise your hands above your head and stretch again. With your hands locked and your arms straight above your head, slowly move your arms to the left and feel your right side stretch. Then slowly move back up to the position above your head and stretch again. Finally lower your arms to the right and feel your left side stretch.

B.) *Legs*

Toe Touches:

1. Stand tall with your legs together and straight. Bend at the waist and touch your toes and hold the position for 5 seconds. Come back up and repeat 3 times. If you cannot touch your toes, reach down as far as you can without bending your knees.

2. In a standing position, cross your legs, keep your legs straight and repeat the toe touching process described above. Then cross your legs the other way and repeat.

3. Spread your legs and move both hands down to the left foot and hold for 5 seconds. Repeat on the other side and then repeat both sides 3 times.

4. Sit on the floor with both legs together and straight out in front of you and do the toe touching process described in #1.

5. While sitting spread your legs apart and do the toe touching process described in #3.

Calf Stretch:

1. Stand facing a wall more than an arms length away. Lean and place your hands on the wall while keeping your feet flat on the floor. Slowly allow your upper body to move closer to the wall and feel your calf muscles stretch for 10 seconds. Repeat.

2. Get on your knees and put your hands on the floor in front of you. Then raise your bottom up high. With your feet flat on the floor and your legs straight form a bridge with your body. Hold this position for one minute.

C.) *Back*

1. Lie on the floor and bring your knees up while keeping your feet on the floor. Place your right ankle on your left knee. Clasp both hands behind your left leg and pull your leg toward you and hold this position for 10 seconds. Repeat on the other leg.

2. Do the exact same thing as #1, but this time straighten the leg you are pulling on so your leg is perpendicular to the ground.

3. Lying on the floor with your knees up, cross your right leg over your left leg. Then slowly bring both legs down to the right. Bring your legs back up and repeat 5 times. Repeat the same process on the left side after crossing the left leg over the right leg.

Chapter Seventeen

<u>Wisdom</u>

In previous chapters I have shared bits of wisdom that I learned from my high school football coach. Because he was the most inspirational coach I have ever known, I would like to share more of his wisdom in this chapter. My hope is that you will be impacted by his messages and will pass them on to others.

<u>Coach L. Marvin Moorehead</u>

"The Pointer Bitch Theory" – Coach reminded us that a female dog struggles to get her first pup out, but after that first one the rest of the litter comes out much easier. He said the same thing was true with touchdowns. Once the first touchdown was scored, the rest came easier. Coach would use this analogy to encourage the offense to go out and score quickly and for the defense to make sure they stopped the other team from scoring first.

A classic example of *"The Pointer Bitch Theory"* is the four minute mile. For decades it was believed that no human could run the mile in less than four minutes. Then when Roger Bannister did it in 1954, the mindset of future milers changed. They no longer believed that four minutes was an insurmountable barrier. Two weeks after Bannister's accomplishment an Australian broke the four minute mark and many runners have followed since then.

Once our minds become convinced that something can be accomplished, barriers come down and achievement is attained. So it is with many things we strive for in life.

"Be Poised" – We were to be poised during the games and when a frustrated opponent would try to pick a fight we were to do nothing but point to the scoreboard. Staying poised in the heat of battle; what a great lesson for all athletes.

"Be Decisive" – Another excellent lesson he taught us was to be decisive. If we ever got up to the line of scrimmage and couldn't remember what to do, he trained us to take decisive action. The worst thing we could do was to stand in a state of confusion and do nothing. Confusion and uncertainty are a part of life. Coach taught us that when those times would come, taking decisive action would be more productive than being fearful and doing nothing.

"Controllable and Uncontrollable Factors" – Coach taught us about the factors we couldn't control in a football game such as the referees, the weather, and the preparation of the other team. Then he convinced us to not spend a second of our time and energy on the uncontrollable factors because to do so was counterproductive. Instead we were to focus 100% of our attention on the factors we could control, most of which could be found by looking in a mirror.

"Be a Mud Thinker" – If it was a rainy Friday night, coach would gather us together and say, "Tonight, we are going to be Mud-Thinkers." It was an effective way to interrupt the negative thoughts that could have developed about playing in the rain. By being "Mud Thinkers" we not only didn't allow the rain to bother us, but we actually embraced it. We started telling ourselves how exciting it was to play in the

rain. "I'm a Mud Thinker", was a statement of defiance not against the rain, but against any negative thought about playing in the rain. Coach knew there would be rain storms in our lives and we would be better prepared if we became "Mud Thinkers".

"No Excuses" – I remember how Coach would never tolerate excuses. If a player was being reprimanded, the one thing that Coach did not want to hear come out of that player's mouth was an excuse. Back then I didn't fully understand why, but I knew for sure to never give Coach an excuse. Now I realize that he was teaching us a very important lesson. To always take full responsibility for our results and to never play the victim role and blame others.

"Intensity Magnifies Size" – These three words were on a sign above our locker room door. This was coach's version of, "It's not the size of the dog in the fight, it's the size of the fight in the dog." None of our guys were very big so we needed to be reminded that we could play bigger than we were if we played with intensity. This lesson made us focus on what we could do with what we had.

"Get Wet All Over" – This was coach's way of expressing the importance of total commitment to the task at hand. If we were going to do something that was important whether it be a block, a tackle, a run, a big game, an exam, a relationship, a job, a life – the best way to get it done successfully was to totally immerse ourselves in it.

Chapter Eighteen

<u>Action</u>

Now that you are reading the last chapter that means you have been through all of the material and have done all the exercises. I trust that you have enjoyed the experience and have found some techniques that have given you a solid foundation for your mental conditioning. There are a few action steps I suggest you conclude with:

1.) Go back to your goal statement that you did in Chapter 1, get out a piece of paper and completely re-write it. Now that you have the benefit of being at the end of this book your goal may be clearer and your reasons for achieving your goal may be even more exciting. Your action steps will probably include many of the exercises you have learned in this book. I believe an effective action plan should include at least the following:

> 1) I will visualize myself achieving my goal for my next event right when I wake up and right before I go to sleep. (Chapter 3)

> 2) I will state my Goal and my Identity statement three times right after I visualize in the morning and in the evening and also before each practice. (Chapter 1 & 2)

3) For more important events I will go to the place where I will be performing and will visualize accomplishing my goal.

4) I will constantly monitor my thoughts and if I detect any doubt or other type of negative voice I will be quick to respond with awareness, laughter, toughness, or kindness until those voices cease. (Chapter 4)

5) To enhance my mental toughness I will work on raising my tolerance to pain. (Chapter 4)

6) When I am performing I will stay in the present moment. (Chapter 5)

7) I will determine what athletes to model and will study everything I can about those Heroes. (Chapter 6)

8) I will develop effective Rituals to do prior to my competition and/or prior to each of my efforts.
(Chapter 7)

9) I will be rewarded when I achieve my short term objectives and my major goal. (Chapter 8)

10) I will expect to perform much better than ever before and will watch my thoughts carefully to assure complete acceptance of this higher level of performance. (Chapter 9)

11) I will monitor my thoughts and my images carefully and if I need some potent tools to get back on track I will use Rewind and Slingshot. (Chapter 10, 11 & 12)

12) Should I feel excessive anxiety, I will know exactly how to feel confident again quickly. (Chapter 13)

13) If I do not achieve the results I expected, I will know exactly how to react so I can improve next time. (Chapter 14)

14) To avoid burnout and to help me enjoy my season I will have rewards for myself (Chapter 8). I will also take time to lift my spirits. (Chapter 16)

15) I will have specific methods to get myself energized and ready to compete. (Chapter 16)

2.) Make it Happen – Taking action is the key to accomplishing your goals. Once you know what you need to do it is time to take decisive action. To help remember the importance of taking decisive action, come up with a catchy phrase. Nike used to have commercials that said, "Just Do It". A motivational writer named W. Clement Stone made famous the phrase, "Do It Now". One of the comedians on Blue Collar Comedy ends his routines with the slogan "Git R Dun". Whatever phrase you choose, just remember to take action and make it happen.

3.) Web Site: For ongoing motivation and for tools to help athletes reach their goals be sure to visit the web site **www.Unleashthechampion.com.**

4.) Feedback: Please email to me your experience with what you have learned in this book and how you have applied it to your sport. It is extremely important to me to know your response to the messages in this book. I can be contacted at **www.Unleashthechampion.com.**

5) The following is the Inaugural Speech given by the President of South Africa, Nelson Mandela in 1994. If you ever want to be inspired by studying the life of a man, your time will be well spent learning about Nelson Mandela. I believe it is more than appropriate to end this book about reaching your full potential with this speech. I suggest you copy these words and put them in a place where you can be continually reminded of the power that lies within you.

"Our deepest fear is not that we are inadequate.
Our deepest fear is that we are powerful beyond measure.

It is our light, not our darkness, that most frightens us.
We ask ourselves, who am I to be brilliant, gorgeous,
talented, fabulous?

Actually, who are you not to be?
You are a child of God.

Your playing small doesn't serve the world.
There's nothing enlightened about shrinking so that other
people won't feel insecure around you.

We are all meant to shine, as children do.
We were born to make manifest the glory of God that is
within us.
It's not just in some of us, it's in everyone.

And as we let our own light shine,
we unconsciously give other people permission to do the
same.

As we're liberated from our own fear,
our presence automatically liberates others."

1994 Inaugural Speech - Nelson Mandela

Appendix A
Suggested List of Music To Lift Your Spirit
 (* shows my top picks)

Song	Artist if known
25 or 6 to 4	Chicago
Ain't Seen Nothin Yet	Bachman Turner Overdrive
A Moment Like This	Kelly Clarkson
Anyway	Martina McBride
Are You Gonna Be My Girl	Jet
Back In The High Life	Steve Winwood
Beat It	Michael Jackson
Believe In You	Touched By An Angel Soundtrack
Born To Fly	Sara Evena
Break My Stride	Matthew Wilder
Bugler's Dream/Olympic Fanfare & Theme*	Leo Arnaud & John Williams
Burning Love	Travis Tritt
Calling All Angels	Train
Celebration *	Kool and the Gang
Chariots of Fire	Vangellis
China Grove	Doobie Brothers
Dance To The Music	Sly and The Family Stone
Dancing On the Ceiling	Lionel Ritchie
Dare To Dream	Jody Messina
Don't Stop Believing	Fleetwood Mac
Dude Looks Like A Lady	Aerosmith
Everybody Have Fun Tonight	Wang Chung
Eye of the Tiger (from Rocky) *	Survivor
Feeling Stronger Everyday	Chicago
Fighter	Christine Agulera
Flying Without Wings	Reuben Studdard
Forever Young	Rod Stewart
Footloose	Kenny Loggins
Free Bird	Lynyrd Skynyrd
Get Ready 4 This	2 Unlimited
Feelin Stronger Every Day	Chicago
Freedom	George Michael
Futures	Jimmy Eat World
Free Ride	Doobie Brothers

Gimme Some Lovin	Blues Brothers
Gonna Fly Now (Rocky Theme) *	Bill Conti
Good Lovin	The Little Rascals
Good Vibrations	Beach Boys
Greatest Love Of All	Whitney Houston
Head Strong	Trapt
Hella Good	No Doubt
Hero	Mariah Carey
Heroes*	Aerosmith
Higher	Creed
Higher Love	Steve Winwood
Highway to the Danger Zone (Top Gun Theme) *	Kenny Loggins
Hurts So Good	John Mellencamp
I Believe	Fantasia Barrino
I Believe I Can Fly	R Kelly
I Can See Clearly Now	Johnny Nash
I Feel Good	James Brown
I Get Around	The Beach Boys
I'm A Man	Chicago
I'm Alive	Celine Dion
I'm Comin	Will Smith
Impossible Dream (from Man of La Mancha)	Mitch Leigh
I'm So Excited	Pointer Sisters
I've Got The Power	
It's My Life	Bon Jovi
Jump *	Van Halen
Jumpin Jack Flash	Rolling Stones
Kryptonite	3 Doors Down
Larger Than Life	Backstreet Boys
Lean On Me	Bill Withers
Life is a Highway *	Tom Cochran
Life Will Never Be The Same	Haddaway
Listen To The Music	Doobie Brothers
Live Your Dream	Charlie Souza
Lose Yourself	Eminem
Love Can Move Mountains	Celine Dion
Macarena	Los Del Rio
Man In The Mirror	Michael Jackson

Mess Around	Ray Charles
Mony Mony	Billy Idol
More Than a Feeling	Boston
Mr. Big Stuff	Jean Night
My Sharona	Cars
One Moment In Time *	Whitney Houston
Pour Some Sugar On Me	Deaf Leopard
Power of Love *	Huey Lewis
Reach *	Gloria Estafan
Ready For This	Dynamic Dual
Ready To Run	Dixie Chicks
Respect	Aretha Franklin
Rhythm Is Gonna Get You	Miami Sound Machine
Right Now *	Van Halen
Rudy (Rudy Theme)	Jerry Goldsmith
R.O.C.K. in the USA	John Mellencamp
Runnin Down a Dream *	Tom Petty
Saturday	Elton John
She's Not Just a Pretty Face	Shania Twain
Skatman	Skatman John
Shake Rattle & Roll	Bill Haley & The Comets
Shout	Tears For Fears
Simply the Best *	Tina Turner
St. Elmo's Fire *	Tony Furtado
Standing Outside The Fire	Garth Brooks
Start Me Up	Rolling Stones
Start The Commotion	The Wise Guys
Staying Alive	Bee Gees
Stronger	Britney Spears
Star Wars Theme	John Williams
Summon The Heroes*	John Williams
Susudio	Phil Collins
Summer of Sixty Nine	Brian Adams
Swing Town	Steve Miller Band
Take It To The Limit	The Eagles
Takin Care Of Business *	Bachman Turner Overdrive
That's the Way It Is	Celin Dion
The Eagle & The Hawk	John Denver
The Contender	Hans Zimmer
The Middle	Jimmy Eat World

119

The Olympic Spirit*	John Williams
The Power	Elton John
The Time of My Life	Dirty Dancing
There You'll Be	Faith Hill
This Is How We Do It	Montel Jordan
Time For Me To Fly	
Turn The Beat Around	Gloria Estafan
U Can't Touch This	M.C. Hammer
Up	Shania Twain
Walking On Sunshine	Katrina & The Waves
Warrior	EMP Project
Wave On Wave	Pat Green
We Are Family	Sister Sledge
We Are The Champions	Queen
We Built This City	Jefferson Starship
What'd I Say	Ray Charles
What A Feeling	Irene Cara
We Will Rock You	Queen
When You Believe	Mariah Carey
Won't Get Fooled Again	The Who
World's Greatest	Art Kelly
You Can Do Magic	America
You Gotta Have Faith	Billy Joel
You're A Shining Star	Earth Wind and Fire
Your Unbelievable	EMF

About The Author

Denny Dicke is devoted to helping athletes perform their best. He is an author, motivational speaker, businessman, coach and former athlete. At Upper Arlington High School he was the starting running back on the football team which won two State Championships. He was also captain of the varsity basketball team. In his sophomore year he won the State Championship in the 400 meters. In his senior year he was State Champion in both the 400 and 200 meters. He became a high school All American by placing third in the nation in the 400 meters. Over 35 years later he still holds his high school's record in the 200 and the 400 meters. At Rice University he focused on track and became conference champion in the 400 meters, was voted most valuable track athlete and achieved All American status. He trained for the Olympic Trials while attending graduate school at The University of Tennessee and completed his training with the Oregon Track Club in Eugene, Oregon. His personal bests in track were: 200 meters 21.5, 400 meters 46.3 (open) 45.5 (relay split), and 800 meters 1:47.9.

Because of his passion for sports and working with young people he found time to coach football, soccer, softball, baseball, basketball and track and field over the last thirty years.

Athletes and coaches benefit from Denny's wisdom and experience and his ability to effectively communicate and motivate.

www.Unleashthechampion.com

Printed in the United States
134201LV00009B/36/A

9 780979 549007